Also by Ja
(Available from Emer

NO SHOES ALLOWED

This is one little paperback we plan to have permanently in the shipboard library. If you've ever chartered, worked on a charter boat, or seen the movie *Captain Ron*, you'll get a big kick out of *No Shoes*.

- Sailing Magazine Latitude 38

In its pages, you can feel the sun shining and those steady winds blowing, hear the lilt of Caribbean English and slip into island time.

- Pacific Yachting Magazine

An unexpected treasure. After being inundated with crime and romance, this is a very welcome change. It keeps the reader on edge and laughing from beginning to end. Offers great material for a TV series!

- Cedar Creek Book Club

Delightful tales in a dream world setting. This book will make even the most serious landlubber want to chuck it all and head for the tropics.

- The Dockside Express

Fascinating, humorous and different. A welcome and uplifting breeze of fresh air. Leaves the reader longing for more.

- Mirrors

The author puts you right there onboard with the good times, the hardships, the sun and wind, and several funny stories that will make you forget your stressful day. He shares his life with the reader which makes him come into your home as someone real.

- John T. Bruere

Gone to Come Back

by

Jan J. de Groot

EMERALD POINT PUBLICATIONS
21909 - 3rd. Avenue, Langley, BC
V2Z 1R8 Canada
Phone (604) 533-7185 Fax (604) 533-7194

GONE TO COME BACK

First edition published 2000
by Emerald Point Publications
21909-3rd Ave. Langley, B.C. V2Z 1R8
Phone (604) 533-7185, Fax (604) 533-7194

Edited by Mike Hendriks
Layout by Karen Young

All rights reserved
Copyright © 2000 by Jan de Groot

ISBN: 0-9683547-1-8

No part of this book may be reproduced or utilized in any form or by any means, electronic or mechanical, including photocopying, recording, or by any information storage and retrieval system, without permission in writing from the author.

If you purchased this book without a cover, you should be aware that this book is stolen property. It was reported as "unsold and destroyed" to the publisher, and the author nor the publisher has received any payment for this "stripped" book

Printed in Canada by Jasper Printing
a division of Quebecor Specialty Group

"I do regret some of the things I have done.

But, most of all, I regret what I have not done."

For Jules

I also dedicate this book to my crew:

To Twin, who has gone back to his native Antigua, and still works on yachts.

To Vibert - JP, who now is a delivery skipper.

To Rudolf - Mankind, still in Grenada, and who is now in the trucking and taxi business.

To Thomas - Steambox, who now lives in the Silicon Valley and is in the computer business.

To Raphael - Canejuice, who has gone to the U.S.A.

To Aubrey - Goblet, who roams the seas working on cruise ships.

To Rochelle - Rock, who operates a taxi business and takes visitors on guided tours in Grenada, and who together with his lovely wife Joan, operates a small restaurant in Woburn, Grenada. There, they spoil their clientele with delicious local delicacies.

Without this terrific bunch of people these times would not have been as enjoyable.

Table of Contents

PROLOGUE

When a West Indian storekeeper leaves his shop unattended and wants to convey to his customers that the shop is temporarily closed, a sign displaying the message 'Gone to come back' is often hung on the door. The sign means what is stated: he or she is gone, but will return. It usually implies that the merchant will return shortly after having been to the post office to mail a letter or having run some other errand. However, there is no guarantee that the absence is of short duration. After all, the clerk at the post office may have encountered a friend in the lineup and there is a need to catch up on some of the local gossip. Or, the shopkeeper meets a friend when returning from his errand and he receives and accepts an invitation to go fishing. In that case the shop may be closed for an indefinite amount of time... it could run into days!

When I left the West Indies after having been there for a period of some ten years, I did not think, nor did I plan, to leave permanently. Heaven forbid! To me those islands are more like home than anywhere else in the world. So, I hung up a sign too. Not on the door of a shop but somewhere inside my head. I could plainly see it whenever I cared to look; the sign read 'Gone to come back'.

This book is the sequel to its predecessor *No Shoes Allowed*. That book has been widely read and pressure was brought to bear by several of my readers to continue. "Surely, it cannot end there? There must be more." That question was fired at me repeatedly. So, when the third edition of *No Shoes Allowed* went to press I made a promise to my readers that there would be a sequel, and this is it!

All of these events, as in the first book, are true accounts. Except for a short period on the coast of the Pacific Northwest, most of the tales related in this book occurred in those wonderful islands in the Caribbean called the West Indies.

These islands, in my opinion, are incomparable to most other areas in the world because of an ideal climate, splendid topography, lush vegetation, steady sailing breezes, and relative short distance from one island to the next. All this makes them ideal for the cruising yachtsman and adventurous traveller. But what makes these islands most spectacular are the inhabitants.

The people who live here come from a mixed background: most are of African descent, some East Indian, Spanish, French, British, Dutch, and some Caribs. As a whole and individually, they are West Indian. They are a unique blend of gracious people, many of whom I feel proud to call my friends, virtually all of whom have made me feel welcome in their home, the islands of the West Indies.

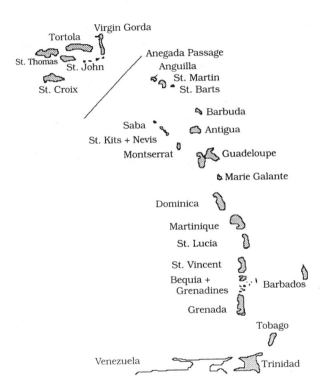

The Islands

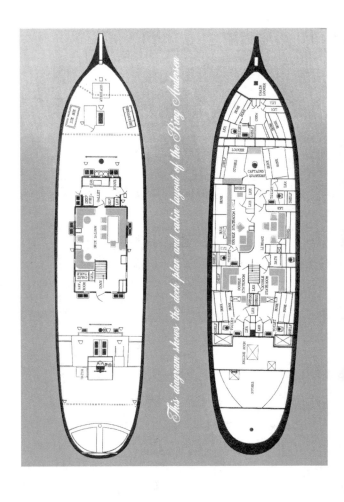

Layout of the Ring Anderson

Sexy Suzie

I couldn't help overhearing Paul's telephone conversation. He stood next to me at the office counter of Grenada Yacht Services.

"I'll take forty five thousand. I need a quick sale!"

For a moment he listened to the voice on the other end, and then I heard him say, "OK", after which he slammed down the phone.

We were about to depart with a charter party that had arrived a few hours ago. I was in the office to pick up my mail and to settle the moorage bill. The next stop would be the Customs and Immigration office located one floor down in the same building. As I gathered the moorage receipt and my parcel of mail, I looked at Paul who seemed to be deep in thought. Paul was the owner of a sailing yacht called *Sexy Suzie*. The boat was built of steel, in Holland, and he had recently sailed her to the Caribbean. The yacht was only about a year old, sixty feet in length and fitted with a lavish interior. One of the most outstanding features was the navigation station. It was equipped with the latest in electronics built into a console that would have done justice to a science fiction space ship. The futuristic layout and its instruments were the fruits of Paul's labour. Paul was a lean and handsome fellow in his late thirties. He was an electronic engineer who had decided to go cruising.

"Are you having a garage sale Paul?" I asked jokingly, referring to his phone call.

"No, I have to sell my boat." he replied.

"You have to sell your boat? Why?"

"That's a long story," he sighed. "Why don't you buy her? It's a good deal, forty five thousand dollars!"

Perplexed, I looked at Paul. "You mean you'll take forty five thousand for *Sexy Suzie*? When I heard you on the telephone, I thought you were selling something else."

"No, no," he replied hastily, "I want that for the boat. That was a boat broker in the States I was talking to. I need the money now, immediately, I can't wait!"

I thought about Paul's response. It didn't make any sense. Forty five thousand? His boat was worth at least ten times that much.

"What gives?" I asked. "That's ridiculous, why don't you borrow the money against the boat? Are you in some kind of trouble?"

"Listen, I'll tell you what's going on. Then you'll understand."

"Go on," I encouraged.

"Well, it's like this. I named the boat after my girlfriend, Suzanne. Together we sailed the boat over from England. When we arrived in Barbados we had a big argument and we broke up. Suzie went back to England."

This was news to me. Paul had been in Grenada for several months and I had never heard of this girlfriend before, but presumably that's why the boat had been christened *Sexy Suzie*.

"I've now met this girl from Argentina, and I want to marry her."

"So? What's that got to do with selling your boat? Does she get sea sick or something?"

"You don't understand. The girl's parents are very rich and very conservative. The fact that I've been living common-law with Suzanne goes over like a lead balloon. The boat reminds them of my sinful past. That's why I have to get rid of it."

I had a strong suspicion that the prospects of marrying into a lot of money had some influence on Paul's haste for an early wedding date, but still...

"Surely you could put the boat up for sale and wait until you can get a decent price for her. After all, that would show your good intentions to the family. Or," I chuckled, "why not change the name? Call it, *Sexy Isabella* or whatever the name of your new girlfriend is. That should pacify them."

Paul was in no mood for humour.

"No, that won't work. I need the money now. It's much more complicated than that." He wrung his hands in anxiety. "You see, I am still married."

"What? To Suzie?"

"Oh, no, not to her. No, I have a wife in England. I need the money to pay her off and get a quick divorce. That's why I need the forty five thousand dollars."

I stared at him with amazement.

"Do you understand now?" Paul said in a desperate tone. "Haste is of the utmost importance. If the family finds out that I was married while living with Suzanne, my chances of getting consent to marry their daughter are zilch. And, without their blessing..."

He did not finish the sentence. The implications were well understood. The prospects of great fortune did play an important role.

"Why don't *you* buy my boat?" Paul said again.

"I would, if it wasn't for the fact that I don't have forty five thousand bucks lying around."

"You can borrow it from the bank. You have been here for a long time. You are established here and as the owner of the *Ring Andersen* you should have no problem raising the money."

The thought had occurred to me. It seemed like one heck of an opportunity to make a fast buck: buy her for forty five and offer her for sale for, say, two hundred and fifty. It should not take long to sell her for such a bargain price. Even if I could flip her for ninety thousand I would still double my money. But there was no time to put it together. Our charter guests were waiting on board. We had to leave. No time to go to the bank and convince the manager to loan me the funds. Heck, even if he okayed it, it would take days to get the paper work finished. While the logistics raced through my mind, Paul was watching me with expectation.

"Sorry, it can't be done. There's not enough time. I have charter guests waiting on board. I have to get out of here."

I wished him well and went into the Customs office to process my departure papers. Twenty minutes later I was back on board where the crew had readied the yacht for sailing.

I had forgotten all about Paul's problem when I settled back into the routine of taking the *Ring Andersen* away from her berth. We soon proceeded through the narrow channel which connects the yacht basin with the Carenage, the main harbour of St. George's, and then went out through the harbour's mouth where we were welcomed into the arms of the blue Caribbean Sea. The sails were raised, the engine was stopped, and *Ring* settled in for her northerly course. My guests were lined up along the starboard railing, taking in the sights of the harbour and the island's magnificent coast line. I also watched as the land slowly slipped by, never tiring of the captivating scenery.

I have travelled to many different parts of the world, but to me, none have been as attractive as the chain of islands lying along the eastern reaches of the Caribbean Sea: Grenada, St. Vincent, St. Lucia, Martinique and Dominica, all belonging to a group called the Windwards. Of all the Caribbean islands I find this group the most spectacular. Volcanic in origin, their mountains rise steeply from the deep blue Caribbean Sea. Located in the sub-tropics, north of the Equator, the climate is warm and sunny, yet cooled pleasantly by the forever blowing trade winds. The fertile volcanic soil, combined with the ideal temperature and rain showers of short duration, gives birth to an abundance of vegetation. The slopes of the mountains, covered with dense forests, display a multitude of shades of green accented by the vibrant reds, soft pinks and creamy whites of the leaves and flowers of the frangipani and flame trees.

Grenada is my favourite of all the windwards. Here, waterfalls sparkle along the mountain sides while the seducing aroma of tropical spices - nutmeg, cloves, cocoa, coffee - loiters through the valleys. Even on the water, on *Ring's* decks, the spicy perfume wafts through the air. Down near the water, the lush vegetation spills toward palm fringed beaches which stretch on for countless miles, displaying their contrast between the blue of the sea and the green of the foliage with a line of pinkish white, coral sand.

We were now leaving Grenada's capital city, St. George's, located on the southwestern side of the island. The city is built against the hills which surround a horse-shoe shaped harbour originating from an extinct crater lake which has long since submerged into the Caribbean Sea. Time has stood still since the city was built. Influenced by Spanish, French and British occupation, the splendid Colonial architecture remains unaltered. The handsome, red roofed buildings rise up against the surrounding hills from a stone walled harbour. Local island schooners tie up here to sell their wares collected from other islands, while spices are loaded to be transported to far away places. Steep, narrow and windy roads curve up from the harbour, meandering their way into the residential areas of the city.

The abundance of tropical growth can also be witnessed in St. George's. Bogainvillea crawl their way up against the walls and over the roofs of the buildings. Palm trees and hibiscus line the harbour front, their many coloured flowers competing with the pastel toned hull sides of the schooners and fishing craft.

On a plateau in the city, overseen by the quiet presence of a stately church, the market place thrives with commercial activity, the open stands crowding each other on the market square. Busses, painted in brilliant colours, luggage strapped on their roofs and named after Saints or cherished loved ones, discharge their tightly packed cargo of shoppers and merchants from the surrounding hills and countryside. Donkeys and carts laden with harvest from the land and the sea come and go, while the sound of reggae music, electronically transmitted from some of the stands, blends in with the cackle of the market ladies.

This island paradise is complemented by a population of gracious people whose unique wisdom and sense of humour are constantly surprising and intriguing. To the newcomer this becomes apparent by their incredible wit when it comes to handing out nicknames. Virtually everyone has one. Once a nickname has been given, that person's real name is soon forgotten and no longer used. There appears to be a general acceptance of this habit. Once a name has been assigned you're stuck with it, like it or not. No one complains, even if the name may sound somewhat unflattering. Nor is it meant in a derogatory way. It just happens to be the appropriate name for that person. For instance, one particular yachtie who had taken up residence in Grenada was physically deformed. He was born with one normal arm and one arm that was considerably shorter. He was promptly named 'De Clock'.

All of my crew were known by their nicknames, although I usually called them by their Christian names, except Twin, whose real name, Laughland, was too cumbersome.

Readers of *No Shoes Allowed*, the predecessor to these ramblings, are already familiar with our seaworthy enterprise and colourful crew, but for those who are new to our operation I will give a brief recap.

My wife Jules and I own and operate the beautiful sailing yacht *Ring Andersen* in the charter business. We take small groups, usually six people, on cruises through the islands of the West Indies. Most trips are one to two weeks in duration. The boat, the *Ring Andersen*, is named after her builder, the famous Ring Andersen Yard of Svenborg, Denmark. Affectionately called *Ring*, the yacht was built along the traditional Baltic Trader lines with some refinements in her finish and a finer bow and rounded counter stern. Her elegant and spacious interior was designed by naval architect Slaabe Larsen. With a total length of nearly 120 feet, a beam (width) of just over 21 feet, and a draft (depth) of 10 feet, she had been massively constructed of oak and beech timbers. The *Ring Andersen* is ketch rigged, her main mast is 98 feet tall and her mizzen mast 84 feet. She carries her 4000 square feet of sail well, allowing her to be comfortable even in the often blustery trade winds.

We have an excellent, all West Indian crew of six, sometimes eight, depending on our schedule. Twin is our gourmet chef. Raphael, better known as 'Canejuice', a name he picked up when caught raising havoc in a rum distillery as a teenager, is the mate/boatswain. Thomas, pronounced with the emphasis on 'mas', is the acting engineer and responsible for starting *Ring's* air-start engine, which coincides with a lot of loud huffing and puffing sounds, hence his nickname 'Steambox', abbreviated as 'Box'. Vibert, commonly known as 'JP' (there was a Justice of the Peace in his ancestry), is our deck hand and later became boatswain. Aubrey - 'Goblet', because of his pigeon-chested posture, is our steward.

Rudolph, the well mannered and friendly deck hand known as 'Mankind', and Rochelle, much easier to say 'Rock', our other deck hand. Then there are 'Ants' and 'Metric' (I don't know their real names), two little guys for miscellaneous chores.

My nickname was originally Copperhead, but that recently changed to Smoothies. Don't ask me why. Jules is Jules, but the market ladies address her as Mrs. Ring Andersen. I have on occasion heard her being referred to as Tenile, probably inspired by 'the Captain and Tenile'.

Our entire crew lives in Grenada, and although *Ring Andersen's* official registry is in Canada, our home port is actually in Grenada. Granada Yacht Services, commonly referred to as G.Y.S., is a marina and shipyard located in St. George's. It is here where the *Ring Andersen* is berthed when not on charter and where we carry out most of the maintenance to keep her in first class condition.

The charter we had booked was somewhat unusual in that most charters go from north to south. We prefer it that way because the sail in a southerly direction is much smoother due to the prevailing trade winds. The reverse trip, south to north, we usually avoid with charter guests onboard, since it can be rough going. This charter, though, had come through the booking agent with the specific request to start in Grenada and end in St. Martin, which lies roughly 400 nautical miles in a northerly direction. The booking had come through Lynn Jachney Yacht Charters. Lynn is a knowledgeable yacht charter broker who knows the Caribbean waters first hand. She would have explained the consequences of the proposed route to the charter guests.

The charter party consisted of three married couples from France. Pierre and Jacqueline actually resided in Tunisia where they owned and operated a large hotel. Pierre was a charming man in his late forties. Marie was very chic and looked to have walked off the cover page of *Vogue*. She seemed a confident woman who felt at ease in any situation. Bernard and his wife Monique were about the same age as the hoteliers. Bernard was a sizeable man, but of the quiet and agreeable sort. He was the President of a prestigious French newspaper. He and his wife also settled in with ease and comfort. The third couple, Antoine and Claudette, were antique dealers. Later I learned from Pierre that both were heirs from wealthy families and their dabbling in antiques was merely a hobby, not a necessity to earn a living. They were both well travelled and, as I gathered during subsequent conversations, well connected with various personages of high society.

This was the group's first charter adventure. They had never been to the West Indies and had never travelled in a sailing yacht, except Pierre, who had done some sailing in the Mediterranean.

About ten days had passed since my conversation in Grenada with Paul, the love struck owner of the yacht *Sexy Suzie*. We had left Martinique behind and were en route to Dominica when Pierre, who liked to take turns at the wheel, confided to me the reason for their charter. It was his intention to purchase a sailing yacht. They had selected the trip northwards because he had heard that this was the roughest passage. He wanted to know what it would be like to sail in choppy water; to find out if he still wanted to buy a boat when the sailing got rough.

They had all taken to the voyage like ducks to water and settled into ship board life as if they had been on boats forever.

"Yes," said Pierre, the wheel firmly in hand, throwing a glance at the compass and making a slight adjustment to the course, "this trip has convinced me that I definitely want a boat."

"Well," I said, sitting beside him on the coaming of the steering console, "they build some nice yachts in France. It shouldn't be difficult to find one you like."

"I already know exactly what kind of boat I want," Pierre said. "I want one of those boats they build in Holland, one of those steel ones, clipper bow, ketch rig, about 60 feet…"

As his voice droned on describing the boat of his dreams, a picture of *Sexy Suzie* started to flash before my mind. Pierre portrayed her perfectly. My thoughts raced from Pierre to desperate Paul. *Forty five thousand dollars! Seventy thousand dollars?* I looked at Pierre, still talking about his dream boat. *Ninety thousand? No, don't push it too far, eighty thousand? No…*

"Eighty five thousand dollars," I blurted out, interrupting Pierre's description of *Sexy Suzie*.

"What did you say?" Pierre looked at me startled.

"Eighty five thousand dollars," I repeated. "That's what that boat can be bought for."

"What are you talking about?" Pierre said. "What boat can be bought for eighty five thousand?"

"Your boat! It's lying in Grenada, one year old, perfect. Exactly what you want! Eighty five thousand dollars and

St. George's Harbour

Fort George overlooking harbour approaches

Rivers and tropical foliage

it's yours, worth at least four hundred thousand!"

I then told Pierre about Paul's urgent need to sell his boat. I figured that if I managed to make the sale I could make some kind of deal with Paul to collect my tidy profit.

"Hm, that sounds attractive. How do we proceed from here? I would certainly like to see it, but when? The boat is in Grenada. We are several days away from there." Questions, questions, questions.

"I'll call Paul on the radio," I said. "Then we'll set up something."

"O.K. Maybe you can do that now? I'll stay at the wheel."

I jumped off my seat onto the deck and trotted to the radio/chartroom, tuned the radio to the right channel, lifted the mike and pressed the send button.

"Sexy Suzie, Sexy Suzie, this is the Ring Andersen. Do you read? Over."

No reply...

"Sexy Suzie, Sexy Suzie, this is the Ring Andersen."

Still no reply. I waited a few minutes, contemplating what to do. Maybe Paul was not onboard, or his radio was switched off. Try something else. Try calling my friend Bert on the yacht *Dana*. I pressed the send button again.

"Dana, Dana, this is Ring Andersen." Instant reaction this time.

"Ring Andersen, this is Dana," my friend Bert replied.

"Hello there Bert. I'm trying to get a hold of Paul. Have you seen him around?"

"No Jan, he left two days ago. I think he's heading north, but I don't know what his destination is. Where are you?"

"We are just coming up on Dominica. We'll be spending the night off Portsmouth, in Prince Rupert Bay. If you find out where *Sexy Suzie* is, could you call me?"

"Sure, will do!"

"Thanks, take care. Ring Andersen out." I hung up the mike, then picked it up again. One more try.

"Sexy Suzie, Sexy Suzie, this is Ring Andersen."

No response.

"Any vessel, any vessel, this is the Ring Andersen. Request location of the yacht *Sexy Suzie*. Standing by, two six three eight."

No reply.

Where could he be? I went back to Pierre who was waiting for my report.

"He has left Grenada, Pierre, but I don't know where he's gone. I'll have to try again later."

"Do you suppose his radio is not working?"

"No, I doubt that. There could be all kinds of reasons. Maybe he is anchored somewhere and gone ashore. Maybe he is on deck and out of range of the speaker. Or perhaps his radio is not switched on. Could be any number of reasons. We'll just have to keep trying; eventually we'll get him."

I took Pierre's place at the wheel as he stepped down from the steering station to join his friends who were seated close to us on the aft deck. Although the entire group spoke English fluently they automatically reverted to French when amongst themselves. From the bits and pieces of conversation I overheard, it soon became obvious that Pierre was explaining the details about the pending boat deal. The words 'bateau' and quatre-vingt-cinq mille dollars were repeated frequently.

Several more times that day and the next day, I tried
to raise Paul on the radio without success. During this
time I observed a remarkable transformation taking place
in Pierre's attitude. Initially, when I first told him about
Sexy Suzie, he was keenly interested, but in a reserved
sort of way. He had wanted to see the boat first and then
possibly make an offer. As time went by he became more
anxious. In fact, I got the distinct impression that he was
suspecting me of wanting to keep the boat for myself.
Toward the end of the second day, when again I tried to
locate Paul without result, Pierre was willing to buy the
boat sight unseen. And he suddenly presented me with a
cheque for eighty five thousand dollars!

"Here, I want to buy that boat, here is the money."

Startled, I looked at the cheque. It was made payable
to me!

"But, Pierre," I exclaimed, "I can't take this. It's not
my boat. The boat belongs to Paul. You'll have to deal
with him!"

"Well, where is he then?"

"I don't know!"

"But he has to be somewhere. How far away can he
be?"

"I don't know Pierre, he can't be too far. He went
north, so he is somewhere between Grenada and us. He
couldn't have passed us. We're several days ahead of him."

"Then let's go and look for him."

"Look for him? You mean turn around and sail back
in the direction of Grenada?"

"Yes, why not?"

"Hm, that could take a long time, but it's a thought."

The others, who had been listening to our conversation, had thus far been quiet, until Jacqueline, Pierre's wife, interrupted.

"Pierre, is that a good idea? Going all the way back? Would it not be easier to go by plane?"

"That's one heck of a good idea," I agreed. We could charter a small plane and check out the anchorages to the south of us. *Sexy Suzie* will be easy to spot from the air."

"Excellent!" said Pierre, as he hugged his wife. "You're a genius!"

"All right then," I said, "if that's what you want, we should go back to Martinique where we can charter a plane. As a matter of fact, there is someone there who I know and who has a small aircraft. He'll probably be willing to fly us around." I was thinking of John and Judy. They used to run a catamaran out of Grenada and had since relocated to Martinique where they were operating an excursion boat, catering to the tourists from the cruise ships. John was an avid flier and owned an aircraft which was parked at the Martinique Airport. "We can be back in Martinique tomorrow. In the mean time, I will try to get a hold of John to arrange for the plane."

Bert and his wife Lenny, the operators of the yacht *Dana* were comfortably seated in the saloon of their yacht. With satisfaction they looked at the multitude of shiny objects occupying the large dining table, various chairs and part of the parquet floor.

"I wonder why Jan is so eager to get a hold of Paul," Lenny said. "He has been calling him for days. Morning, noon and night."

"Yes," Bert answered, "perhaps it has something to do with this stuff." He picked up one of the objects standing on the floor beside his chair. It was a large silver bowl with intricate carvings. It was heavy and undeniably Sterling silver. Several other bowls of the same design, but different in size, were scattered throughout the saloon. The table was covered with forks, knives, spoons, milk jugs, sugar bowls and other items which completed the extensive set of silverware.

"I wonder why Paul was in such a hurry to get rid of it. And so cheap! Five hundred dollars, it's a give away."

Bert did not answer. Instead he stretched his arm, balancing the bowl in his hand, estimating its weight. "You know," he said pensively, "there must be at least a hundred dollars worth of silver in this." Turning the bowl he studied it from different angles. He turned it upside down, looking at its base. Something drew his attention. He moved the bowl closer to get a better look. "There is something written here. Pass me a rag would you. Maybe if I polish it a little I can read it."

Lenny passed him a cloth and found some silver polish. Bert started rubbing as Lenny watched over his shoulder. Then they both peered at it. They could now clearly read what was stamped into the surface of the base of the bowl:

'Property of Cunard White Star Lines.'

Bert and Lenny looked at each other. Triggered by the same thought, they both jumped for the table and started to investigate the other items. Every piece bore the same inscription. They looked at each other, then Bert shrugged his shoulders and said, "Naw, that doesn't mean anything. This stuff is old. They probably sold it when they were refurbishing the ships..."

Bert and Lenny weren't the only ones who fared well by Paul's immediate need for cash. The local dive shop bought scuba tanks, wet suits, regulators, a compressor, and various other related items for next to nothing. Apparently, *Sexy Suzie* had been very well equipped indeed.

Ring Andersen was sailing into the bay of Fort de France. When approaching the anchorage, I decided to try my luck at calling Paul one more time.

"Sexy Suzie, Sexy Suzie, this is the Ring Andersen." Silence. Then a crackle and suddenly,

"Ring Andersen, this is Sexy Suzie."

I couldn't believe my ears. "Paul!" I yelled down the mike, "Is that you?"

"Hello Jan, yes it's me. What can I do for you?"

"Gee Paul, I've been trying to get you for days. I have a buyer for your boat. Where are you?"

"I am in St. Lucia. I have sold her and just delivered her to the new owner."

"What? You're kidding me. Really? You sold your boat?"

"Yes, the whole deal is done, all wrapped up. I am outta here. Booked a flight departing this afternoon. Take care, I have to go now."

Well that was that. My hope of making a quick bit of cash had fallen by the way side. I now had to face Pierre and bring him the bad news. Surprisingly, although disappointed, he took it very well. "Not to worry," he said. "We won't let it spoil our good time onboard. I'll get my boat eventually."

Ten days later we arrived in St. Martin and said goodbye to our guests. The new group that took their place brought us back to Grenada. Along the way, I learned that *Sexy Suzie* had been purchased by a yacht broker in St. Lucia. He sure recognized a good deal when he saw one.

A few months had gone by since the *Sexy Suzie* affair. I was called to the phone while we were doing some maintenance work on *Ring*. It was the editor of a yachting magazine for which I had written some articles.

"Would you be interested in coming to the States to give a talk and do a slide presentation to a Yacht Club? All expenses paid plus a fee for your appearance."

Would I? I was honoured. "Of course. I'll do it. When?"

He gave me the dates and details. Three weeks later I was on my way to the United States.

The audience was great, very responsive and appreciative. There were about two hundred of them. When it was over, several gathered for a chat. One was a man who asked when I was going back to Grenada. When I told him my flight was leaving in the early afternoon of the next day, he asked if I would have lunch with him and if he could drive me to the airport. I agreed.

The next day, George Bradford picked me up at the hotel. We drove to a restaurant, sat down at a table, and ordered lunch.

George, my host, was good looking, well dressed, and had a jovial, pleasant manner. I guessed him to be in his early forties. He told me that he was the branch manager of a local bank. He explained that he had recently bought a sailing yacht. The yacht was in the Caribbean and soon he would be taking extended leave from his job to enjoy his new purchase. He wanted to know about the best places to see, the best anchorages, what to look out for, what were the best routes, and so on. He pulled a chart from his briefcase and spread it over the table. The chart encompassed the area from Puerto Rico to Trinidad. As accurately as possible, I marked some of the highlights. He was delighted with the information I gave him.

"What sort of boat did you buy?" I asked. "And where exactly is she now?"

"The boat is presently moored in St. Lucia. I bought her from a yacht broker there."

"Oh, really?"

"Yes. She's a beauty. Steel construction, 60 feet, bought her really cheap, but I am not too sure about her name. I may have to change it, but maybe that's not such a good idea. They say it's bad luck to change the name of a boat."

"What's the boat's name?" I asked, already knowing the answer.

"*Sexy Suzie*. Do you know her?"

"Yes, sort of," I answered, amazed at the incredible coincidence. I was burning to know what price he had paid for her and wondered how to ask without being told to mind my own business, when he volunteered.

"Oh, you know her. Well then you must know what she is worth. I practically stole her, only paid two hundred and twenty five thousand dollars. Isn't that a fantastic deal?"

I nearly choked. From forty five, if that's what the

broker paid, to two hundred and twenty five. Yes, that certainly was one hell of a deal. Oh boy, why did I miss out on that one! George was looking at me expectantly. He repeated his question.

"Well, what do you think, that was a good deal, wasn't it?"

"Yes, yes, an excellent deal!"

George and I agreed to be on the look out for each other while cruising the islands. He drove me to the airport. We shook hands and said goodbye.

The following charter season was a busy one. I kept an eye out for *Sexy Suzie* and her new owner, George Bradford, but never saw a trace of them. I reckoned that we had missed each other and that George and his boat had left the area seeking new horizons. Eventually, I forgot about the '*Suzie*' incident altogether.

At least a year had gone by since my presentation at the yacht club when we arrived in St. Thomas and went alongside a dock at the Yacht Haven Marina. There, to my surprise, I suddenly spotted *Sexy Suzie*. She was tied up along one of the finger docks. I went over for a closer look, wondering if George would remember me. A man I did not recognize was doing some chores.

"Hello," I said, "is George on board?"

The man looked up from his work with a frown.

"Who?"

"George Bradford."

"Oh, him. The bank man. Is he a friend of yours?"

"Well, no, not exactly, I only met him once."

"Why are you looking for him then?"

"I wanted to say hello and find out how he is getting

on with his boat."

"This isn't his boat anymore. She is mine now, unfortunately."

"Unfortunately? This is a pretty nice yacht. Did you buy her from him?"

"Ha," the man replied with a sneer, "buy her from him? You've got to be kidding. I bought this thing from the bailiff. Your buddy paid for it with money he 'borrowed' from the bank he worked for, except he forgot to pay it back. I have had nothing but trouble since."

"What?" I exclaimed. "I had no idea. He seemed such a decent sort of guy."

The man offered no comment. But I was eager to hear more. I began again, trying to loosen the fellow up.

"I knew the boat when she was owned by her original owner, an English engineer. He brought her over from Holland, where she was built."

"Yeah, well I heard about that too. I'm not so sure about him either. Ever since I've owned this boat I get chased for unpaid bills wherever I go. There are liens against her in all parts of the world. I should have never bought her, she's cost me a fortune so far and I never know what's around the corner. I can't take this thing anywhere without being chased by some creditor, or a bailiff serving papers. The lawyer's fees I've spent by themselves are enough to give me nightmares."

"I'm sorry to hear that." I said, making my excuses and leaving the poor guy with his misery.

So much for *Sexy Suzie*!

Stuff

It suddenly occurs to me that I have to do some back tracking. The difficulty with writing a book containing so many memories is that it is easy to run out of sequence, especially in a case like this where some of my accounts have already been collected in another book. I have to remember that not everyone has read the predecessor.

Also, this is not a novel, a continuous story or an account of one event. This is a collection of several anecdotes which come to mind like the removal of leaves which have fallen from a tree in autumn. Those on top get picked up first, others are hidden underneath.

Each time I thought I had accounted for the last story which I felt worth putting down on paper, another one would come to mind. Often a conversation, a word, a name, will suddenly jog my memory, setting me off on a frantic writing spree, but of course, not necessarily in the right order.

As much as possible I have tried to correct the sequence of events, but I admit I haven't been entirely successful, mainly because I am probably a little lazy and get bored with getting too caught up in the logistics of things. I'm afraid I'm one of those people who likes to write the tale and then get on with the next one.

For instance, thus far I have neglected to mention in this collection that I have two daughters from a previous marriage, Karen and Michele. Karen was ten and Michele twelve years old when their mother and I separated. It was an amicable separation and the girls were given the choice that they could stay either with their mom or with dad. They both decided they wanted to stay with me and my new wife, Jules, which should not come as a surprise. Let's face it, what would any child rather do if they were given the choice of either living in a house in Vancouver and attending school, or living on a yacht in the Caribbean taking a correspondence course and hanging out with the yachties.

Mom and I sat down with the girls and talked things over. There is a lot of difference between a girl aged ten and a girl aged twelve. The two years might as well be ten. A twelve year old fits in easier with the charter clientele than a child of ten. Education was another problem. Karen was still in grade school, Michele was entering high school. When we inquired about correspondence courses, the high school course was easier to deal with. Furthermore, it was tough enough for Mom to lose one girl, let alone two. So, after lengthy discussions we arrived at the following solution: Karen would stay in Vancouver and would come down to the West Indies during summer holidays and Michele would come and stay with us on *Ring Andersen*. She would be enrolled in a correspondence course and go to Vancouver at regular intervals to visit Mom and to write tests and exams. As a result, sometimes we had both girls onboard, sometimes they were both in Vancouver. Most of the time Michele was with us, until the last year when she had to go home to do some serious studying.

I'll never forget that last time when Jules and I took her to the airport and said farewell. I thought this is the end of another part of my life, my little girl is leaving for good. I had a lump in my throat for several days. But I am running ahead of myself again.

When I came back from Canada that first time with Michele, she had not met Jules. It took her a while to get used to the idea that there was another woman in her dad's life. Whenever she saw us sitting side by side, she would immediately come over and join us by plunking herself right between us. Jules handled it well. She never tried to be 'mother'. She knew that would be impossible. Instead, she became a best friend and to this day, both girls regard her as such.

Because of the circumstances, the girls became accustomed to making long trips by airplane. As much as possible we arranged for someone to accompany them on these long flights with transfers at various airports. However, this wasn't always possible. Therefore, if they had to travel alone, we always arranged with the airline that they would be supervised by one of the crew and would be transferred onto the next flight under guidance of one of the attendants. The airlines are excellent in providing this service. Although Michele was two years older than Karen, the surroundings in which she grew up in provided her with lessons not learned in a city and school environment. This we thought to be beneficial and put her ahead of most other girls her age. On the other hand she was behind in those things girls pick up from other kids while living in a big city. Some of those things being fashion and make up, or so we thought.

Michele had gone to Canada for a short visit and was to return with Karen. Phone calls back and forth confirmed that they would be arriving in Barbados on a certain flight at a certain time. Jules was to meet them in Barbados and escort them on the flight to Grenada. LIAT is the local airline. The name stands for Leeward Island Air Transport, locally translated into Leave Island Any Time or, Leave If At All, or, Lost In Alien Territory.

Jules had made reservations for the flight from Grenada to Barbados and return. When she arrived at the airport she was told that there was no room for her on the plane. The alternative was to wait for the next flight out. This would not do because then she would miss the connection with the girls. Jules, in panic, stated her case to the clerk at the ticket counter.

"I have to meet these two little girls in Barbados. They can't travel by themselves. Who knows what will happen to them at that big airport in Barbados."

Soon, her plight and that of the two tiny little girls spread throughout the small community that is the Grenada airport. Everyone became involved, especially the officers of Customs and Immigration who felt it to be their duty to come to Jules' aid. Pressure was brought to bear but she could not get on the flight. In desperation Jules chartered a small plane that would get her to Barbados in the nick of time.

When Jules arrived she waited expectantly for the passengers from the Air Canada flight to disembark. With great relief she spotted Karen accompanied by a tall lady and a flight attendant. *That's strange*, thought Jules, *where is Michele?* Jules waved and the trio came towards her. As

Michele, left; Karen, right, in foreground with friends

From left to right: Part time stewardess Sarah, Jules and Michele

they came closer Jules did a double take at the taller one of the trio. It was Michele! High heels strapped above her ankles, painted fingernails, too much lipstick, two big purple circles of eye shadow, eye lashes sticking out like barbed wire thick with mascara, layers of rouge on the cheeks, and an outrageous dress.

"Are you Jules?" asked the flight attendant.

"Yes," Jules said, staring at the apparition that was Michele.

"I brought you your two little girls," the attendant said and then she whispered into Jules' ear, "She changed on the plane!" With a chuckle she left.

Oh my God, thought Jules, *what happened? What are we going to do? What about those Customs and Immigration folks in Grenada? Me and my two tiny little girls!*

Michele appeared to be quite proud of her new appearance; she wanted it understood that she had learned a thing or two in the big city and obviously wanted to impress upon us that she was now a sophisticated traveller.

Jules approached the subject carefully. "Hm, uh, Michele, did your Mom take you to the airport?"

"Yes."

"Hm, uh, does she know that you are, uh, shall we say, um, dressed like that?"

"No," Karen cut in, "Mom doesn't know, she would have a fit if she did, Michele put all that paint on herself as soon as we were on the plane. That's where she changed into that dress and those shoes. I told you, you look weird," she added, turning to Michele.

"Oh, shut up you little monster," Michele bit in.

"Now hang on, take it easy. Let's have none of that.

Michele, you look very, shall we say, worldly, but maybe it needs to be toned down a little bit. Let's see if we can dim the make-up a little."

The trio disappeared into the ladies room and Jules attempted to scale down the intensity of the make-up. She got some of it off, but the stuff was on pretty solid and there wasn't enough time to make a thorough job of it. Their flight was ready to depart. The shoes and the dress would have to remain where they were.

The arrival in Grenada was a bit embarrassing. The officials looked Michele over from tip to toe, looked at her passport and then looked at Jules. "Is dis one of de children dat you mention, Mistress?"

"Uh, yes," answered Jules, embarrassed. "They do grow up fast don't they?" She quickly ushered the pair into a waiting taxi.

Our permanent crew were Grenadians, but every once in a while we'd take on a stray hand, a roaming yachtie looking for a place to stay and a mode to travel. We have had extra stewardesses onboard such as Naomi who needed a ride to the Virgin Islands, and Corinne a friend of Jules' from England. And Lindy, a Welsh girl who stayed onboard for quite some time. Lindy thoroughly confused the male crews on other yachts because of her uncanny resemblance in features and form with Marilyn Monroe. Another girl was Lizzy who was an excellent chef and took over from Twin when he needed a break. On a few occasions we had a male addition to the crew, such as Ray Metcalf, or Tom de Roos, friends from Vancouver. And then there was Hans!

I should point out here that I expected the same loyalty

and punctuality from these casual globe trotters as I did from my regular crew, regardless of creed or colour. Especially when we were underway, as far as ship's business was concerned, friend or not, duties had to be performed as normal.

Hans was a fellow from Sweden who wanted to see the West Indies. He was a diligent and hard working fellow with one peculiar habit which annoyed everybody, especially Lizzie and Jules. He questioned everything that went on in the galley and would constantly hang around and criticize. His particular interest was garbage and waste. On several occasions he was found going through the trash bin pulling out certain items and questioning why this or that had been thrown out. Hans happened to be onboard when Lizzie did her stint as chef and his antics drove her and Jules nuts. I laughed when Jules related those incidents to me. I would shrug my shoulders and say,

"Don't make such a big deal out of it. The fellow is OK, just a bit peculiar."

The girls were annoyed with his constant nit picking. The tea cup had to filled to just two centimeters from the top, with just so much sugar and so much milk. Instead, they would fill it to the brim or put coffee in it instead of tea, or salt instead of sugar.

Hans liked swimming. Whenever we were anchored, as soon as his work was done, he'd put on a pair of odd looking goggles, dive over the side and be gone. What worried me a bit was his habit of swimming great distances. He would swim way out, far from shore. I warned him about that a few times. On a couple of occasions, when he was well out of sight, I got worried and sent a dinghy out to find him, only to discover that he was still afloat, the goggles staring at us like a fictitious monster from the deep.

His long distance swimming adventures became a problem when we were scheduled to haul out at G.Y.S. for bottom maintenance. The haul-out is a big undertaking and the whole crew is required to pitch in. Promptly at seven in the morning the crew stood at their posts to move *Ring Andersen* to the dry dock. The whole crew, except Hans! I was puzzled and inquired about his whereabouts. Apparently he was not onboard, nor had he been on board during the previous night. His bunk had not been slept in. This was strange, but I could wait no longer: the lift at the drydock was ready and the shipyard employees were waiting for us. Thus, we went ahead without Hans, Lizzie taking over his job of helping to handle the lines. When the yacht was lifted and stood high and dry in the dock I asked around if anyone had seen our absent crew member. I was told by someone that he had been seen at the end of the previous day, going in the direction of Grand Anse beach. That alarmed me. Obviously he'd gone swimming and maybe this time he'd gone too far. I assembled the crew, putting Michele and Jules in one of the shore boats, Lizzie and JP in the other. I told them to take the boats to the beach, one searching the waters off shore in one section , the other combing the other part. The boats set off and left the harbour. I called a taxi and took the rest of the crew with me. We drove along the beach, letting one of them out every mile or so to search the area and ask questions and call in on the various beach side facilities. First Mankind, then Rock, then Thomas, then Metric who I had shanghaied from the dock. I told them I would be driving up and down along the beach front and expected them to report to me the minute they uncovered some information. Nelson drove the taxi, stopping every now and then, allowing me to scan the area with binoculars, keeping an eye on the shore boats.

Jules and Michele had the faster boat and had reached the southern portion of the area to be searched.

"What do we do if we find him?" asked Michele.

"I don't know. We'll have to tie him to a rope and drag him in behind us, I guess. He'll be too heavy to bring onboard, unless he is still alive and can climb in. Or we can yell for help. There are lots of people on the beach."

They fell silent for a minute while the motor pushed the boat onwards.

"You think he's dead?" Michelle spoke.

"Don't know. He's been away for a long time."

A few more moments of contemplation and silence.

"If he's still alive, he'll probably tell us to pour him a cup of tea to just two centimeters under the brim," Michele suddenly said and sniggered nervously.

"Yeah, that'll be just like him."

They both giggled.

"Come on, we shouldn't laugh," Jules said, wiping the grin off her face. "This could be serious."

"Yes," Michele answered, then looked at Jules and they both started to giggle again.

"What's that, over there?" Jules suddenly said, pointing in the direction.

"Where?"

"Over there. Look, I think it's an arm."

"Oh my God!"

Their boat moved closer. It was a branch broken off a tree.

I was on my third drive along the beach when I saw Mankind standing on the road, waving his arms. Nelson pulled over and stopped the car.

"Any news?"

"Yes, Skip, he alright. I just talk to him."

"You talked to him? Where is he?"

"Yes, Skip, he shacked up wid a lady in one of de motels. He making for GYS now. Maybe he dere already."

"What?"

"Yes, Skip, it true."

I had difficulty keeping myself under control.

"Mankind, you go back down to the beach and get the others. Hail the boats and tell them to go back to the harbour. When you find the guys, come back here to the road. I'll have Nelson pick you up." I gave Nelson a nudge and told him to step on it to get me back to the marina.

When I arrived at GYS, Hans stood on the dock with a grin on his face.

"Do you realize what you have done?" I let in to him. "You had us all searching for you. All the work has stopped and here you were fooling around with some chicky baby."

"Yeah, well, I met this girl yesterday. I don't see anything wrong with that. Jeez, you are a guy, you understand."

"I understand alright. You were supposed to be here this morning. The yacht was scheduled to be hauled out, it had all been arranged, and you knew that. I could care less what you do in your spare time, but I won't put up with you having the whole crew and the dockyard on standby just so you can have a roll in the hay."

By this time the shore boats had returned. The search crew got out and came toward us but then stopped at a respectful distance, ears straining, wanting to listen in on the conversation.

"But you managed okay without me," Hans said.

"That's beside the point. But as you say, we can manage very well without you, so pack your backs and get off my ship!"

That last remark, I could tell, was overheard by the listeners, because I noticed them shuffling their feet, nudging each other.

Nothing more was said about it, but the cheerful faces of the three girls indicated I would get no argument from them. And that ended Hans' sojourn aboard *Ring*.

Treasure, a Pigeon, and Other Creatures

The Arawaks were the original inhabitants of the Caribbean Islands. They were said to be peaceful people who were driven to extinction by the Caribs. The Caribs, yellow skinned, slanting eyes and straight black hair, came from the Amazon jungles of Brazil and from there travelled northwards in their canoes. Upon their arrival in the Caribbean, they ate the male Arawaks and, since sexual harassment had not been declared illegal in those days, reserved the women for after dinner entertainment. Large soup pots can still be found on the islands. One is used as a planter at the entrance to the pavilion of the P.S.V. resort. Some skeptics claim that these pots are actually remnants of the sugar cane industry. This theory, to the adventurous traveller, is a bit of a let down and entirely unacceptable. After all, one look at that pot and one can just picture an Arawak sitting in there, slowly simmering in the boiling bouillon, heated by a wood fire that's crackling away underneath. If that pot wasn't used for cooking Arawaks, then surely it must have been intended for making stew of missionaries.

The Arawaks called the Caribs 'Caniba', hence the word 'cannibal'. Columbus and other subsequent explorers had a tough time dealing with the fierce Caribs who killed themselves rather than submit to capture and slavery. Several islands in the Caribbean chain have a steep hill or mountain somewhere called Caribs Leap, so called as a memorial to the last stand or, more appropriately, the last struggle and jump of the retreating Caribs. Fort Duvernette, which is located on a tiny island off the south coast of St. Vincent, illustrates the fear instilled by the Caribs to the western colonials. The guns on the fort are trained inland, rather than toward the sea.

Dominica is the only island in the chain counting surviving Caribs among its inhabitants. During the early part of this century, a Carib reservation was established along the north eastern part of the island. As recent as the year 1930, the Caribs were still an unruly lot and, during an uprising, fought the police with rocks and sticks. The fleeing police force had to call in the Marines who, aided by shells fired from the warship *H.M.S. Delhi*, managed to subdue the fearless fighters.

Dominica, sometimes called the Emerald Isle, looms high and foreboding above the blue Caribbean waters. The steep mountains seem to rise without interruption from the bottom of the sea. Dense jungle covers the mountain slopes. There are tales of voodoo and other mystical practices. The wicked reputation of the Caribs, the stories of sacrilegious practices, and the seemingly impenetrable terrain has sent warning signals throughout the tourist world, causing many a yacht to pass the island at a safe distance.

The guns on Fort Duvernet are trained towards the main island, not to the sea

In the Carib reservation

The island is almost inaccessible but for one reasonably sheltered anchorage located on the northwestern side. The island's port, Rousseau, is unprotected from swells and bad weather and not suitable for yachts. This, I think, is why the island has been left in a shroud of mystery. The fear of the unknown! In fact, I have found Dominica one of the more attractive islands in the chain. The landscape is breathtaking, the fauna, raging rivers, and waterfalls spell binding. The population, despite prevailing gossip, is very kind and hospitable. To the best of my knowledge, cannibalism is no longer practiced.

Prince Rupert Bay is the only good anchorage in Dominica. The bay is horseshoe shaped and reasonably sheltered from the swells. On the west side, the bay is open to the Caribbean Sea. Barbers Block is a promontory at the southern end, and Prince Rupert Bluff, another high outcrop, is situated at the northern point. The town of Plymouth lies to the east in the middle, in the curve of the horseshoe. Our favourite spot to drop the hook is close to and in the lee of Prince Rupert Bluff.

During British occupation, the British Commander heard rumours of an attack planned by the French fleet located in Guadeloupe, the French occupied island to the north of Dominica. The British leader decided that a fort located on Prince Rupert Bluff would be well placed to defend him from the French invasion. Running short of armament he instructed his marines to remove the cannons from some of his warships and place them on the top of the Bluff. The cannons were loaded on a hastily constructed barge, then moved to the shore and subsequently hoisted up the hill, to their planned position. The cannons were heavy and only four or five could be placed on the barge at any one time. Apparently, the marines ran into trouble with the last haul. The barge tipped and the cannons fell into the water.

We had a charter party on board who were young, adventurous, and avid divers. They were very much intrigued by Dominica and had just returned from an enjoyable trip to the Carib reservation. Much to my relief, none of them had been eaten, which again proves my point: cannibalism is no longer practiced. We were anchored in our usual spot, close to Prince Rupert Bluff. During cocktail hour, that evening, I told them the story I had heard about the cannons. Their ears perked with interest. They decided to look for the cannons at first daylight the next morning. Sure enough, in the wee hours of the morning all six of them were lined up on deck, armed with flippers, snorkels, scuba tanks, and other diving gear. The launches were lowered and off they went.

For several hours the party frolicked through the waters surrounding the Bluff. Except for a small anchor, a piece of chain, an empty coke bottle, and a porcelain cup, nothing of significance was found. It was time for breakfast. The dinghy engines were started, the diving gear stowed and back they came to *Ring Andersen*. During breakfast we re-examined the story about the capsized cannons.

"Maybe it's just a fable," one of the guests said.

"Could be, but even if it really did happen, where did the barge capsize?" another said.

"There is so much area that it would take weeks to check it out. Also, if they are there somewhere, they would be grown over with barnacles and all sorts of stuff," a third one commented.

"Not necessarily," I replied. "They might be brass cannons in which case the copper content would discourage growth to a certain extent."

"Is that so. Hm, interesting, but how do we know if they are brass cannons? They could be made of iron."

"That's true," I replied, "but since they are ship's cannons, most likely they are made of brass."

The party had vacated the breakfast table in the salon and we were now gathered on the aft deck. I studied the bluff and tried to imagine what had happened on that fateful day over two hundred years ago. I imagined the sailors and the marines straining to load the cannons onto the barge, towing it with a row boat to the spot were the cannons were to be off loaded and dragged up onto the land. The sailors pulling mightily on the oars and sweating in the tropical sun, slowly making their way toward land, the heavy, cumbersome barge following. Where would they go? Most likely to a point where the incline of the Bluff was the least steep. Where would the barge tip? It could have tipped when they were loading it, but then they would not likely have lost a full load. The story tells that the barge was fully loaded, so, most likely, the barge capsized when they attempted to off load her. In that case, the barge had to have been close to the shore and at a place most strategically located to make the trip up-hill feasible. I explained my theory to my guests who readily concurred with this possible sequence of events.

"What we should do," one of them suggested, "is go out in one of the launches and study the lay of the land from further out. The *Ring Andersen* is too close to the shore to give us a good view of the slopes of the bluff."

The response to this was a unanimous agreement. Shortly, the party was gathered in our biggest launch and set adrift in the Bay.

From a distance we studied the shore profile and decided that the eastern slope of the Bluff was longer and less steep. We all agreed that if we had to haul a heavy object to the top, this slope would be the one to follow. Also at the base, there was a tiny beach, an ideal place to discharge the cannons from the barge. We figured that the barge would have been positioned about thirty yards off the beach to accommodate her depth because of shallow water.

With renewed enthusiasm, we sped towards the designated spot. Two divers went over the side and inspected the bottom under the launch. Soon they came up, exclaiming that the bottom of the bay inclined steeply and that we should move about forty feet closer toward the shore. This definitely had to be the place where the barge had been anchored. I dropped an anchor over the side and floated a diving flag while the entire party took to the water. After about fifteen minutes, one of the divers found what looked to be the nozzle of a cannon, the rest buried under sand, no more than thirty feet away from where the launch was anchored. Soon, another one was discovered in the same proximity, then another and then the remains of a gun carriage. Perhaps third cannon is located there too, but if there was, we didn't find it. Later that day we discussed the possibilities of retrieving the heavy cannons from the sea bottom, but came to the conclusion that this would require tremendous effort and proper equipment. Instead, we raised the anchor and continued our journey contented with the knowledge that we had proven the lost cannon story to be true.

The northwestern end of St. Lucia is shaped vaguely similar to Prince Rupert Bay in Dominica, except this bay is called Rodney Bay, and in the place of Prince Rupert Bluff there lies a small island called Pigeon Island. It is actually no longer an island since it is now connected to the mainland of St. Lucia by a primitive causeway. The island is called Pigeon Island because Sir Rodney, commander of the British fleet, kept pigeons here. He was one of the first individuals to use pigeons for carrying messages. They brought him information about the movement of the French fleet located in Martinique. Sir Rodney's spies scribbled the information on tiny pieces of parchment and attached these to the pigeons who would then deliver the messages to Sir Rodney. This famous naval hero is also reported to be the first to use camouflage in warfare. When he learned that the superior French fleet, under the command of Admiral de Grasse was getting ready to attack him, Sir Rodney ordered his much smaller flotilla to head for Marigot Bay. This bay is located about half way down the middle of the west side of St. Lucia. It is actually a bay behind a bay, the second bay being partly obscured from the first by a narrow peninsula that almost closes the entrance to the second basin. This narrow strip had a healthy growth of palm trees. Sir Rodney hid his ships behind this strip of land and dressed the rigging with palm fronds. When Admiral De Grasse sailed down the western coast of St. Lucia, he was unable to spot the British ships hiding in Marigot Bay and continued on his southerly course. As soon as the French fleet had passed, Sir Rodney gave the order for his ships to leave the bay and fall in pursuit of the French. He now had the advantage of the following wind and could out-manoeuvre the French ships to such an extent that he pumped them full of iron, sustaining very little damage himself.

Maybe it was one of the descendants of Sir Rodney's pigeons that came to visit us one day on our way down to Grenada, for a bird flew around us a few times, hit the rigging, and fell into the water. It was Jules who spotted the bird, desperately trying to keep itself from drowning. Upon Jules' cry for help, we promptly rounded up into the wind, luffed our sails and launched one of the boats. With Thomas at the controls, and Jules and daughter Michele crouched down in the boat, they sped towards the suffering creature. With one big swoop Jules scooped it out of the water and held it close to her while Michele was stroking its head, trying to make it feel at ease. Once back on board, it became obvious the bird was exhausted, thirsty and hungry. We found a box, padded it with shredded newspaper, added a bowl of water and bread crumbs and positioned it in a shady spot. We fussed over the bird until it regained its strength. After three days it looked alert and happy. By this time we were back alongside the dock in Grenada Yacht Services, Jules, Michele and I held ship's council and we agreed that it was time to set the creature free. Jules opened the box, lifted the bird out and set it on the edge of the open box. First, it looked back inside the box as if to consider whether or not it should go back in. Then it cocked its head and peered at us. After a moment it stretched its wings and took a leap for *Ring Andersen's* railing where it paraded back and forth for a few minutes. Squinting its head at us again as if to say, "Well, people, it was nice knowing you, thanks a lot, but I have to go now," the pigeon took a leap and soared off towards the sky. Up and up it went until it was high above our masts. Then it swooped back downwards, circled us three times and took off again, this time for good, in a southerly direction.

The charter yacht *Eudroma*, owned and operated by Bob and Helen Reed, had a dog onboard, a smallish female of the Heinz 57 variety. Named Lizzy, she was regarded by Bob and Helen as part of the family and treated with much love and care. Lizzy was remarkably intelligent and was seen by Bob and Helen more as a child than as an animal. Helen especially would become very upset if Lizzy was referred to as a dog. "Don't say that word!" Helen would say with a hushed voice. "Don't let Lizzy hear you! She thinks she is a person and not a," and she would whisper the letters, "D. O. G." Lizzy was a favourite with all the yachties, especially with our two daughters who were little girls at the time. As soon as the yacht *Eudroma* was spotted in an anchorage or marina, off they would go to say hello to Lizzy and play with her. Lizzy, in turn, loved the girls and allowed them to cart her up and down the dock in a baby carriage, dressed up in a blouse and a hat or scarf. We felt happy with their playmate, too, because although Lizzy was small, she was no wimp or push over. As a matter of fact, she could be out-right aggressive to those she didn't like. This was probably due to some Jack Russell ancestry in her. She played with the girls and she was jealously protective of them. At one time, when some local boys started to tease and annoy Karen and Michele, Lizzy promptly chased them down the finger of a dock. To escape Lizzy's anger, and in desperation, they were forced to jump off the dock into the water and had to swim ashore. I could have sworn I saw a smirk of satisfaction, a look of "that took care of those little buggers didn't it," on Lizzy's face when she trotted proudly back towards the girls.

It seemed logical, that whenever Bob and Helen left *Eudroma* to attend to matters back home in Los Angeles, Lizzy came to stay with us. This often coincided with me having to take a trip abroad to take care of some business as well.

While the yacht was in Grenada, the crew would go home to their families after work. With me away, this left Jules and the girls alone on board. Knowing that Lizzy was there to defend them from intruders gave them and me much comfort. Lizzy, instinctively understanding her important position as guard and defender, at night would position herself by the gangway and growl ferociously at anyone daring to come close.

One night during my absence, Jules had gone to sleep on the aft deck. Lizzy had decided to curl up behind her knees. Suddenly, Jules was woken up by Lizzy who had stood up and was looking attentively at some movement she had spotted on the dock. Following her gaze, Jules noticed someone approaching. By the faint lights on the dock she could see he was a large man, unknown to us. He was clad in cowboy boots, silvery pants, and a tasseled, shiny shirt, and wearing a Stetson type hat, an extremely outlandish outfit for the Caribbean! He slowly came towards *Ring Andersen*. When arriving at the yacht, he was about to step onboard when Lizzy leaped towards him, growling, teeth bared. The guy took one look at the advancing monster and, stepping back, almost fell into the water between the ship and the dock. Regaining his balance, he then ran down the dock with Lizzy in hot pursuit and attacking his legs. The fellow could be seen running out through the main gate, giant steps, as fast as his legs could carry him, arms flaying, his Stetson grasped in one hand. At the gate, Lizzy gave one last growl, watching and making sure the chap was well on his way, and then trotted back to the yacht. When on board, she came over to Jules with a motion as if to say, "There, everything has been taken care of. You can go back to sleep now!"

We all like animals, but onboard a charter yacht it is difficult to have pets. Some guests are allergic to their fur, and while at sea, bathroom time is a nuisance. Michele, however, was especially determined to have a pet on board. The subject had been discussed many times and for a long while I had been able to keep my foot firmly planted down. I was eventually tricked into changing my decision.

We had done some charters in the Virgin Islands and departed from St. Thomas for the long haul down to Grenada. We had no guests on board, and Karen had gone back to Canada to attend school. After the first day and night at sea, far away from land, I began to notice some odd behaviour among my crew. They would occasionally throw me a sideways glance. There was a lot of whispering going on: Michele and Jules were making many visits to the fore deck. More than usual. I began to suspect that I was missing something: something was happening, something I was not aware of. I also had the sneaky suspicion that I was the only one on board who was left out of whatever was going on.

Raphael, (Cane Juice) the boatswain, was at the wheel. I was standing by the port railing, studying the set of the sails. There was a steady twenty knot breeze blowing and *Ring*, all sails set, was swiftly cutting her path through the azure waters, leaving a frothy wake behind her stern. There were no other vessels in sight. Ahead of us, slightly to port, the faint outline of a distant shore could be seen. *Saba*, I mumbled to myself, *we're making good time*. I walked over to the starboard side to check the sheets and blocks of the staysail and flying jib, and walked back to the port side to feel the tension on the running backstay of the main mast. I then compared it to the strain on the lower aft shroud. *Could use a bit of tightening,* I thought, and went forward to call Thomas, Rudolf and Rock. "Let's harden up on the running backstay a bit," I said when I spotted the guys sorting out some lines on the foredeck. It was then, as I happened to glance down through the companionway leading to Michele's cabin, I noticed Michele and Jules sitting on Michele's bunk, playing with something furry.

"What's that?" I said, curiously peeking down the hatchway. Startled, they both looked up.

"It's a cat, Dad." Michele answered, picking up the animal, holding it up. "Isn't she cute?"

"Where did it come from? How did it get onboard?"

"Better tell your Dad the whole story, Michele," Jules said with a chuckle.

"Well Dad, I found it wandering around. It's a stray

looking for a home. I felt so sorry for it that I brought it to the boat for some food."

"When did this happen? I'm sure you didn't find it wandering around at sea!"

"Well no, I found it in St. Thomas a few days ago."

"A few days ago? You mean it has been onboard all this time and you didn't tell me?"

Michele, not answering, cast down her eyes and stroked the cat who now lay purring in her arms. I went down the companionway and took a closer look at the ball of fur. It was the most beautiful and unusual cat I had ever seen. The golden, brownish fur was highlighted with black, diamond shaped markings. A black 'M'-shaped, contour accentuated the eyes. I took the animal from Michele's arms and examined it more closely. I said to Jules, "What kind of cat is this? I have never seen anything like it before. It also seems unusually large."

"It is part margay," Jules answered, "a South American wild cat, sort of like a puma. And the it is a she, although she has been spayed. I checked, there is a small scar."

"Spayed hey? A forlorn stray, looking in excellent health, nice shiny coat, and spayed? Where did you say you found this cat, Michele?"

Michele didn't answer. Instead she looked at Jules, and then suddenly changed the subject,

"We have called her Puddy Cat, Dad... Can we keep her?"

"Well, we don't have much choice. We can't very well set her off in a dinghy, I don't think she knows how to operate the outboard, she'll never make it back to shore!"

"Oh thanks, Dad! That's great. Now we have a cat!" Happily she grabbed the cat back from me.

"What about...," I began, looking at Jules. "That's already been taking care off." She interrupted, "We bought a litter box with all the stuff in St. Thomas."

"Yeah, I bet you did. Just onboard for some food eh?" Throwing her a sideways glance, I went up the companion way to see how the crew had made out with the running backstay.

With Puddy Cat now part of the crew complement, a precedent had been established. From now on we were to have a pet on board.

None of us will ever forget that awful night a few years later when we were back in St. Thomas. We were tied up to the main quay of Charlotte Amalie, a concrete wall along the main street of the city where freighters also tie up to exchange their cargo. The weather had taken a turn for the worse. During that pitch dark night, the wind howled through the rigging. The halyards beat an urgent rhythm against the masts while the rain drove in horizontal sheets past *Ring's* portholes. With the mooring lines complaining and the fenders between hull and dock groaning, we were huddled up inside, hiding from the weather, watching a program on TV.

Suddenly, Jules looked around the salon. "Where is Puddy Cat?" She exclaimed. The cat's absence was unusual because as a rule, she was either settled on a lap or otherwise close by, curled up on a seat. We all got into action, searching the ship. She was nowhere to be found.

"I hope she hasn't jumped off the boat and gone ashore," I said.

"With all that traffic! Oh my god!" Jules and Michele,

now frantic, ran for their oilskins.

"No, you girls stay here. I'll get the crew and we'll go and look for her."

"No, no, we're coming too!"

A few minutes later, all of us were searching the quay, then across the street that was congested with fast-moving traffic. Horns sounded and lights flashed as we dodged the speeding cars. After many hours of searching, Jules found Puddy Cat, wet and mangled, in a gutter along the street. I stared down at the poor creature, a lump in my throat.

"You and the ladies go on back to the yacht, Skip," one of the crew said, noticing our distress, we'll take care of her."

We weren't catless for long.

Just east of the island of Tortola is a bay in which a small islet is situated. The islet, called Belamy Quay, is owned by Tony and Jacquie Snell, who together built a residence and restaurant on it. Tony, a professional entertainer from England, livens up the dinner atmosphere with performances that are widely known and popular among the charter yachts. Tony and Jacquie's establishment became our favourite stop, especially for Michele, when she discovered that Jacquie had a cat with a litter of several kittens. It wasn't long after Puddy Cat's accident when Michele arrived on board with a tiny little ball of fur that was promptly named Belamy.

Belamy had not been onboard for more than a few days when we were tied to the dock at Quay Side Marina in Road Town, the capital and main harbour of Tortola. Our usual dock was not available, so instead of being alongside, we were moored with the bow toward the dock and an anchor off the stern. To get onshore, we had to jump into a dinghy that was tied alongside the boat, push ourselves along *Ring's* hull toward the dock and then climb out of the dinghy onto the dock. It was a bit cumbersome, but due to shortage of space, we had no choice. We were busy cleaning up and preparing for the next charter group that was due to arrive the next day. Michele had been busy helping with the cleaning and had gone ashore to take some garbage to the bins, located behind the main marina office building. When she came back, she was carrying another kitten. It was white with a dark bit at the end of its tail and a tabby patch surrounding the left eye. It looked like a pirate!

"Michele," I said, "where did you get that?"

"Oh, Dad, I rescued it from some kids who were going to set it on fire by the garbage bins."

"What?"

"Really, Dad, they stood there with a can with gasoline, trying to pour it over the kitten. They were going to burn it. I hit one of them and the others ran off. The kitten had crawled under a hedge, it was so scared. It was all caught up in the bushes, so I freed it and brought it here. Can we keep it, Dad? It is so afraid, and if we let it go those boys will catch it again and do awful things to it."

"But Michele, we already have a cat onboard. You know we can't have another one."

"Yes, I know Dad, but can't we keep it at least for a few days, so that I can feed it and make it feel better?"

"OK then, you can keep it here until tomorrow. The charter guests are arriving the day after. It has to be gone before they come on board. Feed it, but in the mean time you go around to the other boats and try to find a home for it. And that's final. No excuses!"

That evening Jules was preparing a little treat for herself. She was looking forward to cooking a fish to be sautéed in the frying pan and succulently served with butter and garlic sauce. The fish had been cleaned and was lying on the galley counter. Jules went to the cupboard to select a frying pan when the new white kitten snuck into the galley. Jules, having made her selection, put the frying pan on the stove and went to grab the fish. Just then, she saw the kitten disappearing out through the galley door, the fish in its mouth.

"Hey you, come back here!" Jules cried, chasing after the kitten.

The kitten took a left turn along the deckhouse, running, with Jules in hot pursuit.

"Come here you little monster! Give me back my fish!"

The kitten wasn't having any of it and took another left turn around the forward end of the deckhouse at full speed, the fish's tail bobbing up and down on the right side of the kittens mouth, the head on the left.

"Come back here!" Jules screamed, trying in vain to catch the thief.

The kitten took another left, this time around the aft end of the deckhouse, still running, but now chewing and swallowing the fish piece by piece. By the time it was about to make its second run around the deckhouse, a few more gulps had made half the fish disappear into the kitten's stomach. Only the tail was still flapping out of its mouth.

"You come back here this instant!" Jules was still chasing.

By now a crowd, watching the spectacle with great amusement, had gathered on the neighbouring yachts.

When Jules, unable to catch the animal, saw the last of the fish disappear into the kitten's mouth, she stopped running, and becoming aware of the crowd she exclaimed, "That cat eats like a pig! It swallowed the whole fish!"

Her words prompted an enthusiastic round of applause from the spectators.

The next day I was on the dock when Michele reluctantly appeared on deck with the kitten in her arms. She was going to take it around to the other yachts to find a suitable home. She climbed over the railing, descended into the dinghy and pushed herself along *Ring's* hull toward the dock. Arriving there, I watched her climb out of the dinghy. Suddenly, the kitten jumped out of Michele's embrace down onto the dock and looked around for a route of escape. Then, looking at *Ring Andersen*, and apparently deciding, that was to be its home. It leaped off the dock into the water. Michele and I both watched with amazement as the kitten swam well over a hundred feet towards the stern of the vessel, where the dinghy line was hanging in the water. It clung onto the rope for a few seconds, and then without hesitation, climbed up and hoisted itself back onboard. When there, it jumped up on the railing, sat down, and without further ado, started licking and cleaning itself.

"Well, I'll be... " I said to Michele. "Have you ever seen anything like it?"

"I guess it wants to stay with us, Dad. What do you think?"

"Oh, all right, I suppose we've got ourselves another cat, and a good sailor to boot!"

And that was the end of that. The new cat was called Piggy.

When taking on a West Indian crew one takes on responsibilities which in North America may be considered beyond the call of duty. However, I didn't mind that. I was fond of my crew; they were an excellent bunch who were prepared to do anything for me. Besides being their Skip, I was also their confidant, family counselor and adviser on matters of importance. If a family expansion was in the works, I was asked how and where to add onto the house. If one of them was drinking too much, his wife or girl friend would ask me to keep a watchful eye over the booze consumption. If an important item for the household was to be purchased, I was consulted and invariably ended up choosing the item at the store. It was therefore no surprise when Rudolph (Mankind) approached me and asked what I thought about him getting a cow. "You see, Skip, dere's not much milk on de island. Most of de milk, she imported and very expensive. I tought if I has a cow, I milk she, and den my family, dey has good milk, cheap."

"But what happens when you're away, Rudolf. Who will milk the cow then?"

"Oh, no problem Skip, de wife she good lady, she know how to milk de cow."

"And what about food: hay, grain, and that sort of stuff? That's expensive! Where would you keep it?"

"Oh, dat no problem too, Skip. We have plenty of space and dere be lots of grass to eat."

"Well, then, Rudolf, I think it sounds like an excellent idea."

I thought that would have been the last of it, unless I was expected to go to some cattle auction to pick out the right cow. In that case, I could offer little help since I know as much about cows as I do about picking the right number for a lottery ticket.

A few weeks after Rudolf's question, we were anchored in Carriacou, an island to the north of Grenada. We were in full charter trim and had a party of four charter guests onboard. They were two couples who had sailed with us on *Ring* several times. The guests were on shore and I was watching a local schooner hoisting cargo on board when Rudolf appeared by my side.

"I bought de cow, Skip!"

"You what? Oh, yes I remember. So you bought a cow. That's great Rudolf, and is she giving you milk?"

"No, not yet Skip. Dee cow, she not home yet."

"Oh, I see, when is she coming?"

"Dat be depending on you Skip."

"What do you mean, depending on me?"

"Well, you see Skip, de cow she here in Carriacou, I tought we could take she home on *Ring Andersen*."

"You've got to be kidding. A cow onboard? We have guests, Rudolf, are you out of your mind?"

"But Skip, de guests dey's nice people, dey don't mind."

"How do you know that? Of course they mind, and in any event, I mind! Jesus, Rudolf, I tell people to take their shoes off so they won't scratch up the varnish and the decks. What makes you think I would let a cow roam around our decks, depositing manure all over the place?"

"But Skip, I will keep she tied up, on de foredeck, and I clean up after she."

"No way, Rudolf, read my lips, No! It is out of the

question!"

Disappointed and puzzled by my outburst, he stared after me as I made my way to the aft deck where I filled Jules in on the latest development. She burst out in laughter. "You, know," she chuckled, "you should have said yes, then I could have had that horse I've always wanted. It would have been only one more animal. Surely you don't have any objection against me having a nice dressage horse onboard. Would be great for the guests too, they could go riding on the beach. We'd be the only charter yacht in the Caribbean offering sailing and horse back riding, all in one!"

I looked at her with suspicion. I know she was kidding, but probably not quite. Horses were a weak point with Jules, as I found out later. She now has three, but they're on land and not on my boat.

My first introduction into the equestrian world was in San Juan, Puerto Rico. The *Ring Andersen* was in St. Thomas. We were in a panic to repair one of the engine bearings which was badly worn. The bearings were huge and heavy. The bearing surface was made of babit, a relatively soft, metallic material that needed to be re-poured and machined. For this we had to go to a foundry and machine shop in San Juan. I had removed the bearing from the engine, ready for shipment to the foundry, and decided to turn the trip into a businessman's holiday, the holiday being the suggestion of Jules and Michele since the timing coincided with my birthday. The foundry was told to expect us on the chosen date and we hurriedly made last minute travel arrangements with the local airline company.

The company operated seaplanes of the Grummend Goose variety. A reliable source informed me that these planes date back to the Second World War. We had seen them take off regularly but never flown in them. The cumbersome machines would take off and land in the harbour, often barely clearing the masts of the anchored yachts. They could be seen taking off, lumbering to slowly gain speed in the water, and then finally breaking loose from the surface to gradually gain altitude.

We lined up at the ticket counter along with the other passengers. When our turn came, the attendant said that they were short of space. Looking at me he said, "Would you mind sitting with the pilot?" "No, not at all," I answered. Satisfied, the clerk checked our baggage, including the carefully packaged bearing. We proceeded to the boarding platform where the plane was standing.

These planes are amphibious and have wheels which fold into the fuselage when they enter the water. The pilot sat me down in the seat beside him. When I was seated, he started to fiddle with the controls and said,

"Are you a yachtie?"

"Yes, how did you guess?"

"You don't look like a tourist and your tan gives you away."

"Oh, I see."

"Yes, I spotted you at the ticket counter and asked the clerk to ask you to join me in the cockpit."

"You did? Why?"

"Well, you see, I need you to give me a hand. Normally I have a co-pilot, but he is sick today"

"Shit… you're kidding. You got the wrong guy. I know how to run a boat, but I know nothing about flying."

"That doesn't matter, you don't have to fly, I'll do that. I just need help with the pump."

"The pump? What pump?"

"This pump here," he pointed to a handle beside my chair. "The hull of this old crate leaks like a sieve, and when we take off it scoops up a lot of water. Makes the plane too heavy for lift off. So, it has to be pumped out until we are airborne."

I looked at his face to see if the guy was having me on. But no, he was dead serious.

"Is this normal?" I asked

"Yes, it is for these old wrecks!"

"All right, let's go then!" I sent a quick prayer to the appropriate authority and double checked the clasp of my seat belt.

With a roar the two engines came to life. The plane shuddered and shook as it stood on the platform. Then the pilot released the brake and slowly we started to roll down the ramp into the water.

"Start pumping!" the pilot yelled to be heard over the engine noise. "Faster!"

The adrenaline pulsed through my body, and I pumped and pumped as I had never pumped before. We were now speeding through the harbour. I could feel water spraying up from the floor.

"Faster, faster!" The pilot yelled again. I was almost breathless.

"Hurrah! Up she comes. We made it! You can stop pumping now. If there's any water left, it will drain out by itself. Thanks a lot, you can relax now!"

We made it to Puerto Rico without further complications.

"When are you coming back?" the pilot asked as I stood up from the seat to disembark.

"In a couple of days," I answered.

"If it's on my flight, come and see me, then we can do it again!"

I waved and jumped on to the tarmac, thanking my guardian angel for her generosity. Jules and Michele were waiting for me on the platform.

"That was a pleasant flight," Jules said.

"Yeah, sure," I mumbled. "Let's go and get our luggage."

That same day we took the bearing to the foundry and left it there with instructions for the work to be carried out. They promised to have it ready the day after tomorrow. The three of us checked into a hotel, and Jules and Michele started searching through the yellow pages of the telephone directory.

"Guess what," Jules said, "for your birthday we are going horseback riding. You'll love it!"

The next day, early in the morning, we arrived at a ranch where about a dozen horses stood already saddled up. A group of people were milling about, some on horses, others waiting while a chap dressed in cowboy gear was directing the operation. Upon our arrival, he looked us over and selected three horses, one for Jules, one for Michele, and one for me. "I have never ridden a horse before," I said, "so give me something old and tired." "This one will be fine," the man said, and gave the horse a friendly pat on its behind. I watched Jules and Michele climb into the saddle and followed their lead. Once seated, the man came back and adjusted the stirrups. Then the man climbed on his horse and manoeuvred it into a position where he could survey the whole group.

"Are you all comfortably seated?"

Everyone nodded obediently.

"Okay then, we will go for a twelve mile ride to a place were we will stop and rest for a while and get some refreshments. After that, we will circle back to the ranch. The whole ride takes about five hours. I will lead, you all stay well behind me. Any questions?"

No one answered.

"All right then, let's go."

His horse started to move to the front of the procession and we were under way. My horse automatically followed. Jules was in front of me, Michele behind. For the first fifteen minutes everything seemed to be copacetic, but then, as we went down a hill, the party picked up speed and my horse started to trot. This I found to be an outright uncomfortable movement. I was bumped up and down and I swayed left and right and had difficulty staying in the saddle. Suddenly, my horse passed Jules' horse and then the next and then the next. I pulled on the reins because I thought that would make it stop, but it didn't, instead it went faster. For self-preservation I had now let go of the reins and was holding on to a knob on the saddle, with both hands. Then one of my hands slipped but I got a hold of the horse's mane and hung on for dear life. The horse raced on until we passed the cowboy on the lead horse. "Stop!" he yelled. "You are supposed to stay behind me." Thankfully he spurred his horse on and pulled up beside me and somehow managed to stop mine.

"You should stay behind me," the fellow said once again.

"Don't tell *me* that. Tell this *horse*. He is a speed maniac!"

"Yeah well, I know, he likes to be up front."

"Great! That's just what I need, a race horse. I told you, I've never ridden before."

"Just say, Ho, and pull in on the reins a little, then he will slow down. Let's go. I'll take you back to the end of the line."

When arriving at my previous position, there was no sign of Jules or Michele. Looking further back up the road, I saw Jules slowly coming down the hill and Michele further back, parked on top of the hill. The cowboy went to investigate. For a brief moment he stopped to talk with Jules and then continued up the hill toward Michele.

"What's going on?" I asked when Jules approached the group.

"This mare has shoes on all four feet and she slips on the pavement. I have to go down this hill very carefully."

"Oh, I see. But what is the matter with Michele?"

"Her horse doesn't want to go at all. It keeps stopping."

"Wow, that's the horse the fellow should have given to me. I have a heavy duty racing machine here!"

After a short wait, Michele and her horse, lead by the cowboy, rejoined the party. Somehow, with lots of Ho Ho's from me, and stops and giddyups from Michele, we made it to the refreshment stand without too much trauma. Jules' horse was okay once we were on flat ground and had left the pavement. With a sigh of relief I managed to dismount and settled myself into a chair. After an hour, the horses and the people had been replenished with water and drinks and we were ready for the next leg of the voyage.

"How long is the next ride?" I asked our commander.

"Oh, not far. We'll be back at the ranch soon. All mount please!" he yelled to the cavalry, turning away from me.

With a sigh I stood up and climbed once again onto my steed. To my surprise, the animal behaved rather well this time. *Perhaps I'm getting the knack of it.* I thought. *This animal is beginning to understand who's boss, after all!* But, I had spoken to soon. As we neared the ranch, the beast suddenly took off, paying no attention to my Ho's and Ha's. I was hanging on to the knob on the saddle again. We passed the lead horse and kept going. Gallop, gallop, I began to slide sideways in the saddle. Once again I grabbed hold of the animal's mane and hung on for dear life. Then we came to the gate. The horse took a left turn into the drive leading to the barn. It took the shortest route, jamming my left leg between its body and the gate post. Ouch, that hurt! A few more leaps and then it stopped at the barn. Painfully, I let myself slide the rest of the way down to the ground. Thank God the ordeal was over. Except for some bruises on my left knee and leg, I was still in one piece. Never, ever, I swear, will anybody get me back on a horse again!

Orphee, those Magnificent Men and their Flying Machines, and the Revolution

The yacht *Orphee* is a 91 ft. ketch. If my memory serves me right, she was built in Italy by the Sangermani yard. The first time the yacht appeared on the Caribbean scene she was owned and operated by Captain Carlos. Carlos, a tall and handsome fellow, was born in Barbados. His dark features bore evidence of his Spanish heritage. How exactly Carlos had managed to obtain ownership of the beautiful yacht *Orphee* only Carlos knows, but it is apparent that it had a great deal to do with Carlos' charm amongst the ladies.

At one time, *Orphee* was owned by an Italian Countess who had become a widow. The yacht had become too much to handle for the Countess and Carlos had somehow managed to convince her to put the yacht into his care and custody. We can only speculate about what the Countess received in return for the transfer of ownership. The reason why it is believed that the exchange was made under somewhat unusual circumstances became apparent when the Countess decided to come and visit the West Indies and go for a sail on *Orphee*.

Ring Andersen was tied up alongside the dock at G.Y.S. *Orphee* had just returned from a trip and was moored a few spaces behind us. We were in for a few days of maintenance and a well deserved rest from a busy charter schedule.

The crew had gone home and Jules and I were sitting on the aft deck with a tall cool drink when I spotted Carlos approaching our boat on his way to *Orphee*. When he was just about to pass us I called, "Hey, Carlos, come and join us for a drink."

He stopped and looked at us. Then, as if torn with a big decision, his gaze switching between *Orphee* and the drinks on our table, he wrung his hands and said uncertainly, "I don't think I have the time."

Carlos' behaviour indicated that he was under some kind of strain.

"Come on," Jules said, "have a drink. You look frazzled."

"Oh, okay then, just a quick one," and he hopped on board. Settling himself into one of the deck chairs, he wiped his forehead with a tissue and picked up the drink which Jules put in front of him.

"What's going on?" I asked. "You look as if you're being chased by the devil. Something wrong with the boat?"

"No, it's worse than that. The Countess is here and I have a lady onboard who has booked a charter."

"Just one lady who booked the whole of *Orphee* for a charter?" Jules exclaimed. "Wow, Carlos, how did you swing that? She must be rich. Is she good looking too?" she added speculatively while nudging me.

Carlos threw us a devious grin, "Yeah, hm, not bad," referring to the lady's looks, and maybe her money, "but the problem is that the Countess is here too, and she wants to go out sailing as well."

"And you can't take them both, I guess," I commented.

"Oh no, shit no, that would be a disaster."

"Well," said Jules, "If the lady has booked the boat she is entitled to it. What has that got to do with the Countess. She no longer owns the boat; she can't just show up and demand to go cruising if she hasn't made a booking."

"It's not that simple," Carlos sighed and took another sip from his drink.

"Why not?" I asked. "Makes sense to me."

"It's one of the conditions of the sale. I told her that she could come on the boat anytime she wanted."

"Oh," I said, not knowing what else to say. Obviously the Countess believed that she still owned the boat and perhaps a little bit of Carlos too, which would explain why Carlos' single female charter guest was a problem.

"What are you going to do now?" Jules asked.

"Well, somehow I have to keep them both happy. Neither one knows that the other one is here. The Countess is staying in the Secret Harbour Hotel and my charter guest is safely tucked away onboard. I have told the Countess that *Orphee* has mechanical problems, and I will tell Erica the same."

"Erica?" I quizzed, "not Miss or Mrs. So and So?"

"Yes, Erica, my charter guest." He threw me a speculative glance, "We have known each other for a while." He put down his drink and added, "I better go, somehow I've got to keep them both happy." Off he went.

During the next three days we observed Carlos frantically commuting between *Orphee* and the Secret Harbour Hotel. Occasionally, when we saw him, he would throw us a quick "So far so good." Then he would sigh, shake his head and hurry on his way. On the fourth day we had to leave to pick up a charter party in Martinique. Upon our return I learned from Carlos that on the fifth day the Countess had become suspicious and had arrived at *Orphee* for a surprise visit. The result was that both ladies had packed their bags and departed from Grenada in great haste. Carlos shrugged his shoulders and laughed. "I guess I won't have to worry about those two anymore."

Carlos had problems maintaining the yacht properly and he put her up for sale. When a prospective buyer arrived at the scene he quickly poured cement in the bilge to cover an area that was in questionable condition. The trick worked and the boat exchanged owners.

Carlos was absent from the charter scene for a while until he re-appeared with a large motor yacht called *Fair Carol*. One of his charters was with the well-known pop group the Beatles. Fame had apparently gone to their heads and Carlos was not enjoying their demanding ways and obnoxious behaviour. When, after having put up with their antics for a few days, they told Carlos that they did not want his crew to swim on the same side of the boat as they were swimming, this having something to do with contamination of the water, Carlos told them to pack their bags and get off his yacht. Perhaps the disgruntled group put a curse on the yacht, because shortly thereafter, *Fair Carol* sank in deep water. Fortunately, Carlos and his crew managed to save themselves. After that, he gave up boating and bought himself an airplane.

Carlos still kept in touch with the yachties and on many occasion he would call us on the radio. The first time this happened was when we were en route from St. Vincent to Grenada. The radio crackled and then there was this call:

"Ring Andersen, Ring Andersen, you are looking good! Having a nice sail? This is Carlos."

I picked up the mike and scanned the horizon. Not a boat anywhere in sight.

"Hello, Carlos, where are you calling from? Where are you?"

"Close by, I can see you, tuck that flying jib in a little bit."

I couldn't understand it, again I looked around, but there was no other vessel anywhere to be seen.

"Look up, look up, I am above you."

And then I saw and heard him. His plane dove and made a circle around us, tipping its wings in salute. Ever since then I became accustomed to looking for Carlos in the sky whenever he called on the radio.

Orphee's new owner installed Soona, a fellow from Sweden, as the new skipper. He and his charming girl friend Shenagh, assisted by a good crew, ran the boat in an efficient and professional manner. We readily became good friends with this amiable couple. After a period of chartering, some of *Orphee's* deficiencies started to get to the point that an extensive refit was required. *Orphee* went north to have the work carried out.

We hadn't seen *Orphee*, nor had we heard from Soona and Shenagh for nearly a year, when we sailed into the harbour of Gustavia in St. Barts and spotted the yacht lying at anchor. The boat looked incomplete. Some of her standing rigging (wires supporting the masts) was missing, and especially her main mast stood sort of forlorn and lonesome with only the minimum of support. Her booms were lying on deck and the sails were nowhere to be seen.

When *Ring's* anchor was lowered and set, I went into the dinghy, clearance papers in a briefcase, and set off for Customs and Immigration to take care of the formalities of ship, passengers, and crew for entrance into the French island of St. Barts. The first person I saw when I was about to enter the Customs building was Soona. Briefcase under one arm, he had apparently just completed the task which I was about to begin.

I was delighted to see him. "Soona, how the hell are you? Great to see you. Saw *Orphee* in the harbour. Where have you been, where are you going?" My excitement was silenced by Soona's somber reply.

"Jan, I'm sorry, I can't talk now. I have to go; I'm in a hurry. Good bye. Say hello to Jules."

Dumbfounded I stared after him as he quickly made his way towards the quay where his shore boat was tied up. Shrugging my shoulders I entered the building and started the clearing process. When I came out, I saw *Orphee* leaving the harbour.

Jules and I discussed the strange encounter at length

but could not come up with a plausible explanation. What was also puzzling was the obvious un-seaworthy state of *Orphee's* rigging. We could not understand what possessed Soona to take the yacht out to sea in such condition.

Some months later we were in St. Thomas and looked up our good friend Jeannie Raaphorst. We had known her for a long time. Originally we met when she was onboard a trimaran owned by her sister and brother-in-law. Jeannie is a lady with many talents. Besides being a gourmet chef, she also has excellent secretarial skills. Her culinary talents were much appreciated when answering a call for help on any of the charter yachts. Her secretarial skills came into play during her employment at the posh PSV resort. When we met in St. Thomas she was employed in a boutique selling up-scale jewelry. Later, she became well known in the charter industry when she started an employment agency for yacht crew placement in Fort Lauderdale. Jeannie now resides permanently in Fort Lauderdale and hires out on luxury yachts as a chef on short terms.

We were delighted to welcome Jeannie on board *Ring* for dinner during the first night of our arrival in St. Thomas. As we exchanged news, our encounter with Soona and *Orphee* came up. Much to our surprise, we learned that Jeannie was onboard *Orphee* at time of the incident.

"You're kidding," Jules said, "you were on *Orphee* when she was in St. Barts?"

"Yes, of course," said Jeannie. "We saw you sail in and anchor, but we were too far away to be heard. We couldn't come over because Soona didn't want us to leave the boat. Also, Soona didn't want us to talk to anyone, because he was afraid it would be found out where we were going."

"Then what the heck was going on?" I asked.

"You won't believe me if I told you."

"Try us," Jules and I both said.

From her French mother Jeannie had inherited the tendency to illustrate her stories with an abundance of hand and arm gestures.

"Okay then, here it goes, but be prepared for one of the weirdest situations you could possibly imagine." With a laugh, she spread both arms to welcome us into her tale.

"You knew that *Orphee* needed a lot of work done?"

"Yes, that's why she left Grenada, she was going somewhere up north to get a refit."

"Yes, well, some of the work included overhaul of the rigging and also the installation of a new generator. I joined *Orphee* in PSV shortly after she left Grenada. Eventually, we ended up in St. Thomas where we were to get the rigging renewed and a new generator installed. The work was being done by Baron von Ripoff. You know him don't you?" Jeannie's right hand swung out past both of us demanding confirmation.

We nodded our heads. Baron von Ripoff was the nickname of a German fellow who operated a rigging and machine shop in St. Thomas. One of his hobbies was flying and he had an old, single engine airplane which, by the looks of it, dated back to the First World War. It had an open cockpit and the Baron could be seen sitting in it with his goggles, scarf and leather head gear, the strap loose at the chin. When in his flying machine, he imagined himself to be one of those World War One flying aces.

"Well, yes," Jeannie continued, "the work was not progressing to Soona's liking and the generator was not installed properly and giving constant problems. When the Baron presented one of his outrageous bills, Soona refused to pay him and the Baron got mad. Soona consulted with the owner of the boat and was told that he, the owner, would sort von Ripoff out, and instructed Soona to weigh anchor and leave St. Thomas. We were supposed to go to Miami," Jeannie waved into the general direction, "but Soona decided to first go to St. Barts because there he could get the various parts necessary to complete the rigging. So, we snuck out of St. Thomas and set course for St. Barts. It was kind of scary, especially in the Anegada passage, because the masts were not properly supported. With every swell, the main mast would swing from port to starboard and back again." With her arms above her head, Jeannie imitated the motion. "I felt certain it would break and crash down on the deck. Fortunately, we had good weather and calm seas, so nothing broke, thank God." Her right hand slapped to her forehead.

Jules and I nodded in agreement and urged her on to continue.

"We had left at night. Apparently von Ripoff had gone to a lawyer and filed for seizure of the boat on account of non payment of the repair bill. When daylight came we were already a good distance away from St. Thomas and closing in on St. Barts. At about noon we spotted this airplane circling and cavorting above us. It was Baron von Ripoff. He was throwing things at us from the plane."

"Throwing things? What kind of things?" I was

picturing the flying ace flinging hand grenades at *Orphee* and her crew.

"We didn't know what the objects were. They fell into the water and seemed to float, but they were too far away to identify until, when he made yet another turn and flew over us again, this item landed on the deck.... It was a book." Jeannie's hand emphasized the point when it hit the table.

"A book?"

"Yes, a book. We couldn't figure out what he was up to either, but then it suddenly dawned on me: he was throwing the book at us! You know, throwing THE BOOK! It means something like I'm arresting you, fining you, or whatever."

"Oh, of course," Jules repeated with a chuckle. "He was throwing the book at you, literally! The guy must be daft."

"Yes, but Soona, being Swedish, didn't understand the English symbolism. When I explained to him what the fellow was trying to do or say, he panicked and decided to pick up the parts in St. Barts and leave again as quickly as possible. He was afraid von Ripoff might land there and try to seize the boat. So, as soon as we arrived, Soona took off for the ship chandlers, bought the parts, cleared customs, and we took off again. From there we went to Anguilla, worked like crazy to get the rigging secured, and then went to Miami. When we pulled in there, the boat was seized." Jeannie threw up her hands in despair.

With open mouth Jules and I both gazed at Jeannie and then went over the story again and again.

We never found out how the argument was resolved, but shortly after the incident the yacht changed owners again.

Vast amounts of money had been spent on *Orphee* when once again she arrived in Grenada after having been absent for nearly two years. This time the boat was operated by skipper Perty Tarvas and his wife Debbie. The crew were predominantly American, having signed on in the U.S. When they arrived in Grenada they had returned from a trip to the Mediterranean. The boat was not available for charter and used exclusively for trips by her owner and friends.

Perty was a short, chunky, and serious fellow who kept very much to himself. He was from Finland and quickly nicknamed, 'The End'. British born, Debbie, in contrast, was petite and slim with long curly red hair. Her vivacious personality soon made her popular amongst the yachties. It was quite apparent that Perty and Debbie were not a good match and after a year of disharmony they decided to part company. Perty left for destinations unknown and Debbie stayed on the boat as mate, awaiting the verdict of the yacht's owner.

I should mention here that Debbie was a very capable young lady who could perform any of the tasks onboard with ease. Although slight of build, she was deceptively strong and a well experienced yachtie who was equally at home with the yacht's machinery as with any of the other onboard equipment. When it came to overhauling an anchor winch or scraping, painting, varnishing, or completing mechanical work to the engine, she could do as well, if not better than any experienced sailor. She was also an excellent navigator and capable of running the boat under all circumstances. The logical solution for the owner would have been to make Debbie the skipper and leave the boat in her capable hands. But a female skipper on a boat of that size was a bit unusual in those days, so we expected that a new skipper would be arriving in due course. This made Debbie's position on board rather insecure.

Ring Andersen was going through a period of maintenance. We were getting ready for the new charter season. Everything was to be newly painted, cleaned, varnished, greased and oiled, sails mended, outboard motors serviced, all those things that are required to keep a yacht in top notch condition. I was just about to climb onboard after I had collected the mail from the office when Debbie came down the dock.

"Jan, have you got a minute?"

"Sure Debbie, what can I do for you?"

"*Orphee's* owner just called me, he would like to send some of his friends down for a cruise, but he hasn't found a skipper yet. I told him that you were off charter for a while and might be available to skipper *Orphee*."

"Oh, I see. How long is the trip?"

"Two weeks."

"Hm, well, I have to think about that. Let me talk to Jules, and I have to go over the new work schedule. I'll let you know in a little while."

"Great, I hope you can make it. I'll be waiting for your answer."

Orphee's new owner was no stranger to me. I had met him a couple of times when he was on the boat. He had also been on *Ring* for a dockside visit.

I discussed Debbie's request with Jules and Michele and went over the work schedule. Jules and Michele decided they could cope very well on their own for a while and as far as the work was concerned, everything was well in hand. The majority of the jobs were just routine and best left to the crew to deal with. J.P. who was our boatswain at the time, was fully qualified to sort out any snags if necessary. Another thing not to be overlooked was the fact that the job would bring in some welcome cash which couldn't come at a better time. Maintenance schedules have a habit of gobbling up a lot of money, especially with a boat the size of our beloved *Ring Andersen*.

So, the decision was made. I conveyed the news to Debbie who immediately ran to the office to call the boss. Two days later I waved goodbye from *Orphee* and we departed for Martinique where we were to pick up the owner's friends.

Orphee's crew now consisted of Suzan, a tall and attractive young lady from Canada, who served as stewardess and deck hand, her boyfriend Nick, second deck hand and also a Canadian, much smaller and slighter than Suzan, and Ingrid, the chef from Germany.

A few hours into the voyage proved that Debbie worked well with the crew and had everything under control. I sat back in the helmsman seat and relaxed.

The owner's party was not due in Martinique until a few days hence so we made a couple of stops along the way and dropped the hook in Baie de Fort-de-France well before their arrival. So far I had thoroughly enjoyed the trip and the crew's camaraderie. Skippering *Orphee* was turning into a pleasure cruise rather than a job.

Debbie and I donned our uniforms and took a cab to the airport to meet the guests. They were two couples in their late fifties who had been onboard before. They

Orphee *and* Ring *sharing a dock.*
Debbie tries to improve my appearance.

greeted Debbie with fond memories from previous trips and somewhat reluctantly acknowledged the yacht's new captain. They started to mellow towards me a little bit after they were settled onboard with a couple of drinks, but during the entire trip it was evident that there was a strong bond with Debbie. They quite rightly felt that *Orphee* belonged with Debbie, not with me. During subsequent conversations with them I re-emphasized this attitude by throwing in, at appropriate times, that Debbie was perfectly capable of running the yacht without another skipper, hoping that the message would be relayed to the owner.

The journey proceeded without any notable incidents until we arrived in Bequia. Rumours were going around that there had been a revolution in Grenada. As we worked our way further down the island chain, stories about the coup became more and more gruesome. I was in intermittent contact with Dave Saville aboard his yacht *Golden West*, which was berthed in G.Y.S. His boat had a powerful radio. He managed to fill me in on some of the details. David assured me that all was well on *Ring Andersen*. With great relief I was eventually able to make contact with Jules. Apparently, due to on going work, the antenna had been disconnected but was now temporarily rigged to make contact. Jules also told me that all was well and there was nothing to worry about. Guards had been posted around the marina to protect the inhabitants. Yet, when we arrived at Union Island, a tourist at the bar of a local hotel gave a horrifying report about his escape from Grenada while dodging grenades and gun fire. The road to the airport was strewn with the mangled bodies of innocent citizens. Buildings were on fire and the airport was under siege. Only a miracle and great bravery on his part had allowed him a narrow escape in a private plane. I listened to his story and wondered if it was true or merely an exaggeration. I had heard stories like this once before: at the time Grenada went independent, some years before. Horror stories told at that time by the press were all a figment of the reporter's imagination. I couldn't believe it. It contradicted everything I had heard from Jules and David. Or could it be that the reports from David Saville and Jules had been censored. Were they under surveillance?

We were destined for Grenada but our guests had heard about the coup and people on shore had told them that is was dangerous. Yet my wife and daughter were in GYS, in the middle of St. George's, the capital, the seat of government. I had to get there by hook or by crook. All flights to and from the island had been canceled. The only way to get there was by boat. It was time for action.

I called Debbie and asked her to assemble the crew. I explained my predicament, our responsibility to our passengers, and the boat which did not belong to us. We discussed the pros and cons and the rumours we had heard on shore and my conversations with Dave Saville and Jules. The yacht flew a British flag and was therefore under the protection of the U.K. I didn't think the revolutionaries would want to risk waging a war with England. I new Maurice Bishop, the fellow who had instigated the coup. He was a well respected and a non violent man who, I am certain, had acted not out of malice but in the best interest of the people. I could not see him giving orders to attack yachtsmen and tourists.

It did not take long to make a decision. All of the

crew unanimously agreed that we should go to Grenada and that *Orphee* was to be our mode of transportation. Realizing that the yacht was my responsibility, I weighed all the possibilities and decided that I would make initial contact with the regime from outside territorial waters and proceed with caution. I relied on our British ensign. Now we had the passengers to deal with. I expected they would want to return home from Union Island or St. Vincent.

The party was gathered in the salon. Debbie and I approached them and explained the situation. Again we went over all the gossip we had heard including my personal contact with Jules and David, and my feelings about Maurice Bishop. I told them that we had decided to proceed to Grenada but that we could make arrangements for them to disembark prior to our departure. To my surprise they immediately informed me that they wanted to come with us. In fact, they were looking forward to it. It was an unexpected adventure.

Early the next day we left Union Island and set course for Grenada. When we approached the island we stayed well offshore as we sailed down the west coast. St. George's is situated along the west coast in the southern area. We were approaching from the north. I constantly scanned the coast line with binoculars for signs of unrest. The tourist who claimed to have made his narrow escape had talked about fires: houses burning, grenades exploding. I failed to notice anything unusual. We passed a few small local fishing boats. The fisherman didn't seem to have much concern with the onshore activities. They waved to us as usual. When we were parallel with the harbour of St. George's I called Fort George on the radio.

The answer came almost immediately. I identified the yacht and asked for permission to enter the port. The voice told me to stand by and wait. After a few minutes delay I was told to approach the harbour entrance but to wait outside. We did as told and luffed our sails with the engine slowly clicking over. About a mile offshore we waited. We were poised to trim our sails and engage the engine in case we needed to make a fast escape. I knew that the only navy type vessel the country possessed was a decrepit old tub that would not be able to overtake *Orphee* with all sails set and the engine at full ahead.

Anxiously we waited until we saw the familiar vessel, identifiable by its enormous cloud of exhaust smoke, appear from behind the ridge on which Fort George is built. Our crew stood at the ready at the sheets of the sails. Debbie was behind the wheel with her hand poised on the engine controls. I studied the Grenada Navy's pride and joy with the binoculars as it came putt-putting in our direction. I could make out six men, all of them dressed in army fatigues and carrying rifles. They were hanging onto the side of the deckhouse of the craft as if ready to jump. It didn't look good. I told the passengers, who were standing on deck, to go inside and signaled to the crew that we might have to make a run for it. Then, in the door of the wheel house of the approaching vessel, I saw a familiar shape. I concentrated the binoculars on this person and recognized him. It was the bulky figure of Mr. John, the customs officer. He stood there in his uniform with the usual briefcase containing his coveted official papers. "Relax guys and gals," I said to the crew, breathing a sigh of relief, "it's Mister John. I'm sure they are not going to harm us. If he is onboard it means they have full intentions to clear us in."

As the reception committee drew closer Mr. John waved at us in recognition. I saw him talking to the other men on the boat and pointing to us with a grin on his face. A few moments later, the party came alongside. Mr. John stepped on board and was followed by the soldiers who brandished their rifles in rather an alarming fashion. They told everyone to step on deck and started to search the boat. As they went below, Mr. John whispered to me, 'Don't worry skip, dey is just showing off, no harm will come to you.' I thanked him for telling me and secretly hoped that none of the rifles would go off accidentally because the professional quality of the 'soldiers', in my opinion, left something to be desired. Three of the warriors couldn't have been much older than sixteen. Two of them I knew. They were regular hang arounds at the docks in the marina.

They had completed their search inside the boat and reappeared on deck. I could tell that their behaviour was frightening the passengers. I decided that they had been onboard long enough and needed a bit of reasoning. I told them that I wanted to talk to them and asked them to follow me to the foredeck. When they were gathered around me I said, "You guys are heroes; you have freed Grenada from the oppressive government."

They glowed with pride. One of the two dock rats answered, "Yes, Skip, we is soldiers now. We gonna make Grenada good for de people."

"That's good," I said, "but you don't want to scare off the tourists, because they help the people earn money. The passengers I have on board like Grenada and the Grenadian people, otherwise they wouldn't have wanted to come here during a revolution. I am certain Mr. Bishop will agree with me." That last remark did the trick.

"Yeah, da's true Skip, dey must be good people," one of them said.

"Right, so now that you have done your job here onboard, why don't you go back on your patrol boat and let Mr. John take care of the paper work. We'll go on ahead into the harbour and will take Mr. John with us. That way you can take the patrol boat and be ready if any enemies of the new regime want to get into Grenada. You must stay alert you know."

"Yes Skip, dat's a good idea Skip, we'll do as you aks," said one of the older characters, "Come you men, let's go." They promptly picked up their rifles and climbed back on board their vessel. With a roar and a cloud of black smoke the engine was started and the boat took off.

"How did you do that?" one of the guests asked.

"It was easy," I laughed, "I made them feel important and convinced them we are on their side."

When we entered the harbour we had a good view of the city which is perched against the surrounding hills. I carefully scanned the buildings. There was no sign of destruction. The road surrounding the water was a beehive of activity: business as usual. Above us, on the Fort, I could see some soldiers hanging about. They seemed to be watching us proceed through the entrance, showing no more than casual interest. No cannons or firearms were directed at us. We entered the narrow passage leading to the lagoon in which the GYS marina is located. A young boy wearing an ill fitting uniform was waiting at the dock where we were to tie up. He was awkwardly dragging an Lee Enfield rifle of World War II vintage. The weapon was heavy and out of proportion with his small frame. He dropped the weapon down on the dock as he helped take our lines. Then Michele and Jules appeared, cheery faces, welcome back, everything was fine. As the three of us started to walk to *Ring Andersen* the soldier stepped in front of us, "Hi Skip, you no recognize me?"

I looked at him, "Jeez, Ants! What are you doing in that outfit?" The uniform, much too big for this little guy, the beret way too large and sagging over his forehead and ears, disguised him almost beyond recognition.

"I is a soldier now, Skip," he said proudly.

"What do you intend to do with that big rifle?" Jules interjected.

"I is protecting de likes of me, I mean, de likes of you," he corrected himself hastily.

"Let me see it," I said, taking the rifle from him and giving it a cursory inspection. "This thing is loaded and the safety is off!" I exclaimed, "Do you realize it is dangerous to carry a rifle this way?" I showed him. "Look, this is the safety, turn it this way to lock the mechanism, if you don't it may fire at the slightest jar or when the trigger is accidentally caught. Better yet, take the cartridge out and put it in your pocket." I showed him how to release the magazine and stuffed it into one of his pockets. I gave him back the rifle and with difficulty he slung the strap over his neck with the rifle hanging in front of him.

"No, no, not like that, put it over your shoulder, like this. I arranged the rifle behind him putting his hand on the strap. "Now, hold on to the strap and pull it downwards, that way you can march around and you won't have to worry about shooting yourself into your foot or worse."

"Thanks Skip, now maybe I'll be a corporal soon." With that remark he paraded off, baggy trousers hanging from his tiny waist, beret sagging over his ears.

"Phew," I said to Jules and Michele. "Is that an example of the revolutionary forces?"

Later I was filled in on the details. The coup had been quick and effective. The only casualty had been a man who had tripped over his rifle and shot himself in the leg. No grenades, no fires, no mangled bodies. Sir Eric Gairy, the Prime Minister, had been off the island when the coup took place. The event had been well timed. A few shots had been heard, probably scaring the conquerors more than the attacked. They had entered the radio station and announced that the island was now under jurisdiction of Maurice Bishop. The vast majority of the island's population were on his side: even the police force had welcomed the new regime with open arms. Only isolated incidents were reported, none of which had caused bodily harm.

With *Orphee* safe and sound back in Grenada I returned to my chores on *Ring*. In Grenada things went back to normal. LIAT resumed its regular flight schedule and visitors came and went unhindered.

There was phone call for me at the office of GYS. When I picked up the receiver I heard the voice of *Orphee's* owner at the other end.

"Jan, I have another party coming down, some business acquaintances. They will be arriving in Grenada tomorrow. Have the boat ready for them and take them for a two week trip. I'll leave it to you to give them a good time. You don't have to pick them up at the airport. They know where the boat is. They should be there around three in the afternoon. I've got to run, bye!"

Before I had time to open my mouth the line was disconnected. Dumbfounded, I stared at the phone still in my hand. Slowly I put it back in it's cradle. *What's going on? The fellow must have decided that I am the new skipper.* I trotted off to *Orphee* to find Debbie. She was onboard. I told her about the Boss's phone call. She almost doubled up with laughter.

"Yep, that sounds just like him. He is used to getting his way."

"Well, that may be so, but not with me he isn't. Who the hell does he think he is? Give me his phone number, I'll call him back and tell him."

With the number written on a piece of paper I went back to the office and called the operator. Direct dialing was not yet available in Grenada. When the connection was finally made I was put through to the man's secretary.

"No he is not available; gone out of the country. Won't be back for another five days. Can anyone else help? He will be checking in with us in two days. Would you like to leave a number?"

"Never mind," I said, "I'll call back later."

What now? I turned to Debbie who had accompanied me to the telephone. "He is gone, won't call back until the day after tomorrow."

She said, "That's a day after the guests arrive. It's going to be awkward with them sitting on the boat not knowing what's happening."

"That's right, awkward is putting it mildly."

Debbie and I started to walk back to the boat. "Let's have a coffee and think this over," I said, looking at my watch. "It's just about that time."

We climbed onboard *Ring* and filled Jules in on the latest developments.

"Why don't you do it?" Jules said, "It's only another two weeks and the work on *Ring* is progressing well. There's nothing going on that the crew can't handle."

Debbie looked at me hopefully. "Yes, why don't you? It would solve all our problems. Otherwise, I'll be sitting here at the dock with a group of grumpy people onboard."

I looked from Jules to Debbie, considering their suggestion.

"Okay, let's do it, but we have to talk to the guy sometime during the trip to make him understand that I can't keep doing this. This is the last time. We must get a hold of him and explain to him that he has to make other arrangements. I have my own boat to run."

The next day we set off on yet another cruise on *Orphee*. Several attempts were made to contact the owner. Finally, some time during the second week in the trip, Debbie spoke with him and explained the situation. When Debbie came back onboard she said that everything had been sorted out.

"How?" I said. "What is he going to do?"

"I don't know. All he said was, 'Don't worry about it, I'll get it all sorted out'."

When we arrived back in Grenada, the guy was standing on the dock, watching us come in. He greeted our guests then greeted the crew and us and seemed quite cheerful. When the initial formalities were over he turned to me and said, "Let's have a little talk." We went to the Patio bar at the marina, sat down and ordered a drink.

"Look," he said, "I want you to stay on as Skipper."

Here we go again, I thought. "I can't, I just can't."

"Why not? Is there something wrong with the boat? Is there a problem with the crew?"

"No, of course not. The boat is fine and the crew is great, but I have my own boat, *Ring Andersen* and I have charters starting. I can't run both boats at the same time."

"But what am I going to do? I need a good skipper."

"You have a good skipper. Make Debbie the skipper; she'll do a better job than anyone else you could possibly come up with."

"But she is a girl!"

"So what? She knows the boat inside and out. She is a very competent skipper in all respects. She has the confidence of the guests we have had on board. Believe me, you can't find a better person for the job."

He was quiet for a few minutes, contemplating, moving his glass round and round over the smooth surface of the table. He looked up and said, "You really think so?"

"Yes, I know so. You won't regret it."

He pushed his glass around the table some more and then said, "Okay, Jan, thanks, I think that's good advice. I'll do as you suggest."

We shook hands and I went back to *Ring.*

A few hours later Debbie came by and announced that she was the new skipper of *Orphee.* Michele, who was now nearly seventeen, joined her as occasional crew. I knew she would be well looked after with Debbie at the helm. That night, the *Ring* and *Orphee* contingent celebrated.

As far as I know, Debbie was the first female skipper of such a big yacht on the Caribbean charter scene. She remained on *Orphee* for several years until the boat was sold yet again.

As time progressed things started to deteriorate in Grenada. The new regime was worried about reprisal. Rumours started to spread that Sir Eric was on his way with a large army to re-take the island. It was feared that arms would be smuggled into Grenada to help stage a counter attack. Any shipment coming in was carefully scrutinized and it even started to affect the yachties.

Jack McKitrick was an Irishman who, by his own admittance, had received his formal education while riding shotgun in the back of a bread truck.

Jack was a skipper who preferred to stay in port so that his work would not interfere with his skill at the pool table. Somehow he always managed to find a skippering job on a yacht that needed a refit. As soon as the work was finished he would leave the boat, telling the owner to find another skipper. He was pretty smart that way and never had to venture too far from his favourite pool table. Jane, his girlfriend and a close friend of Jules, was even smarter. She didn't like to cook meat since she was a vegetarian. The odd time that Jack could find no excuses and had to take the boat out with owners or guests, he had to do all the cooking while Jane was comfortably seated, having a good time with the guests.

Jack loved to spring practical jokes on unsuspecting targets. He once conned Jules into letting him teach her how to become a diver. He put so many weights on her belt that when she jumped in for her first lesson, she sank like a stone. It took two onlookers to retrieve her from the bottom. Jack thought this was very funny and couldn't stop laughing. Because of the tense situation in Grenada, the cards were turned and Jack had to pay for his sins.

The yacht *Kalizma*, formerly owned by Elizabeth Taylor was originally skippered by Peter Davis. Although I prefer not to be reminded of the outrageous role I played in the occurrence, readers of *No Shoes Allowed*, the predecessor to this book, may remember an incident involving this yacht and my daughter Michele.

Peter had since left the yacht, and now his position had been taken over by Jack McKitrick who immediately convinced the yacht's owners that a major refit was required.

The refit involved a complete overhaul and refurbishing of the yacht's interior. The project took many months, but eventually arrived at the stage that new furniture was ordered. The shipment arrived and the furniture was moved onboard. The items had been securely packed in rigid chunks of styrofoam. This material was discarded in a large waste bin situated on the premises of GYS. Subsequently, one of the soldiers had started to rummage through the garbage bin and came walking down the dock with three pieces of styrofoam. I was standing on the dock, conversing with some of the other yachties when the man approached us and showed us the items he had in his hands. He pointed out that the imprints in the material resembled the shape of rifles. We studied the objects and agreed that probably that's what is was, packing material for fire arms. Then he asked us if we knew where it had come from. We all immediately pointed to *Kalizma* and suggested he interrogate Jack McKitrick. A crowd of smiling faces stood by as Jack was hauled off to jail. "That's too bad Jack. Don't give up hope, we'll think of you. Stiff upper lip, we'll come and visit, if they let us!." Poor Jack was detained for two days before the matter was resolved and he was released from his confinement.

Maurice Bishop, the new leader of the country, had the best of intentions and tried hard to rule the State in a manner that would benefit the people. However, he was handicapped by a group of power hungry individuals who he had needed to help him gain power. Things started to get out of control as the group's power over him increased. Cuba started to play an important role in the island and later we witnessed a strong Russian presence. A missile base was being constructed under the veil of it being an airport. Political slogans and talks on the radio and newspaper made derogatory remarks about the Capitalists from the West. We began to feel uncomfortable. Slowly, several of the yachts who had made their home in Grenada started to leave. Some of the expatriates who had homes on the island pulled up stakes and moved away.

On several occasions I discussed the situation with my Grenadian crew and expressed my concern. I felt that Grenada's location was of strategic importance. From here, it would not be difficult to raise havoc with traffic to and from the Panama canal. Its location was also a threat to the Venezualan oil fields, refineries, and bulk stations in the Netherlands Antilles, and to Trinidad. I could not imagine how the USA could tolerate a strong, Russian presence on Grenadian soil. I felt that if things didn't improve, the Americans would invade to get rid of the Russian presence with the chance of the Grenadian people getting caught in between.

Little did I know at the time how accurate my assumption was. When sometime later war broke out, the U.S. decision makers were ridiculed for their action. It was said that the Russian presence and missile base was untrue and a tale trumped up to justify the U.S. cause. We knew that this wasn't so. The arrival of Russian ships unloading armament and equipment was a regular occurrence during the dark hours of the night and could be plainly observed from our point of vantage at GYS. Maurice Bishop was pressured into this activity. He didn't, nor did the Grenadian people, want to be subservient to Cuba or Russia. Mr. Bishop tried to stop the culprits in his government and was brutally murdered by his devious allies, much to the horror of an overwhelming majority of Grenadians.

We all know what happened next. The island was invaded by the American forces in a united front with some of the other islands. Peace has now been restored and the island has reaped certain benefits. There is now a much improved telephone system. Now there are traffic lights and cable television. Beneficial? I'm not convinced. I certainly think Grenada could have done without the cable television and the traffic lights.

Sonja

The weather in the Caribbean isn't always as advertised in the brochures. Many an unsuspecting romantic imagines one's sailing boat gliding serenely through the sea with the palm trees waving gently along the shores, while the soothing sound of rushing water parted by the ship's bow is accompanied by the beating of native drums in the distance. Although the weather in the region is generally quite stable, the passages between the islands are nearly always lumpy, the winds coming steadily from the north east, and strong, close to twenty knots. When going to windward, add to that the speed of the boat, and what have you got? A mighty stiff breeze!

Sometimes, things go haywire. The wind builds up to around forty knots, violent squalls rip through the area and the sea is whipped into a frenzy.

It had been a tough trip for Dan and it wasn't over yet. North bound from Trinidad with a full cargo on board his small island freighter *Sonja*, and slugging through rough seas, he had finally managed to work his way toward the leeward shore of St. Lucia. He had had some relief from the unusually strong head winds when he passed the lee shores of Grenada and St. Vincent, but as soon as he had cleared the northern end of those islands, the full force of the wind together with breaking seas, had returned with a vengeance. Now he was approaching St. Lucia and soon the ocean should flatten. He stood alone on the bridge of his little ship. The crew was asleep below, resting from their turns on watch. Dan had hardly any sleep since they left Trinidad two days ago. He was tired and looked forward to a night's rest in Castries, the capital and main port of St. Lucia.

Dan had been a journalist in his 'previous' life. Although he had elected to go to the sea by running a freighter, he was considered to be one of the 'yachties'. He had purchased the ship in Europe, brought her to the Caribbean and had engaged her in the local, general cargo trade.

Most of his present cargo consisted of construction material, such as bags of cement, used for the building of the Hess Oil complex in St. Lucia. *Sonja*, the freighter, was Dan's pride and joy. She was about a hundred feet in length. Her hull sparkled in white paint and was maintained to a standard that put many a pleasure vessel to shame. Dan was assisted by two competent crew who were native St. Lucians.

The Hess Oil facility was being built in St. Lucia due to a quirk in U.S. law. Previously located on the U.S. administered island of St. Croix, the company had been forced to move because they were unable to deliver the oil to the United States unless they used American tankers. The Jones Act stipulates that cargo moved between American ports cannot be carried by ships with a foreign bottom. This means that the ship had to have been constructed in the U.S. and must fly an American flag. The higher freight rate would have put the company out of business. The result was the move of the plant to St. Lucia which created a great boom to that island's economy.

The weather worsened as another squall approached. Sheets of rain enveloped Dan's ship. The wind howled through the rigging of the masts and cargo booms, shaking the wheel house. Dan peered through the window in front of the steering station into the dark, wet night. He tried to find a light on the distant shore or perhaps the outline of the island, but the visibility was so poor that he could barely make out the bow of his own ship. He stood there in the night with feet apart, both hands clamped firmly onto the spokes of the wheel, his tired eyes peeking through the rain slashing against the windows, the electric wiper barely capable of clearing the glass, when suddenly he thought that he saw a movement on the foredeck. Just then, the bow of the ship rose and fell as it encountered a big wave. When the bow came down, an enormous amount of water crashed over the foredeck. As the water poured down the decks and then gradually dispersed through the scuppers, Dan saw it again. This time a bit closer and by the port railing. Something was moving along the decks, slowly making its way towards the aft deck upon which the wheel house was situated. Anxiously, Dan peered through the glass, the 'thing' began to take shape as it approached. It was alive and large! Not an object, but something that moved by its own volition. Slowly moving along the rails, holding on and stopping when the next wave crashed over the ship and then continuing when the vessel rose and shook the water off her decks. Through the window

A local fishingsloop

Dan stared, into the shadows of darkness, taking advantage of each short period of momentary clearing of the glass by the wiper blade. The creature was getting closer, then he lost sight of it as it disappeared below the windshield, under the wheel house, a blind spot, not visible from Dan's position. Suddenly, he heard a noise on the stairs leading to the wheel house, the clanging sound of footsteps on the iron steps. Shivers ran along Dan's neck and his hair stood on end when suddenly the door was thrown open and the creature appeared in the door way. Unable to move and speechless, Dan stood and stared apprehensively at the apparition which seemed to have arisen from the depths of the angry sea.

Slowly Dan began to realize that he was looking at a man, a large black man. Dripping wet and in torn clothing, the man stood in the door way, breathing heavily, exhausted, holding on to the door frame with both hands. Dan stirred to life and with a shaky and shrill voice yelled out,

"Where the hell did you come from?"

The man took a deep breath and with apparent discomfort replied, "You... you ran me over!"

"I what? Ran you over? What do you mean?" Dan exclaimed.

"I was fishing in my boat and you ran me down. My boat, she gone, I grab on to your anchor and climb on board."

And that is how it happened. No small feat. The freighter had hit the fishing boat head on, the man had managed to hang on to one of *Sonja's* anchors which always hung ready in the hawse pipes. He heaved himself on board while the ship was slugging through the heavy seas.

It is not unusual for the local fishermen to wander off, way out into the open sea, in their small, dory type little craft. Their seaworthy little boats, operated with great skill, allowed them to survive even in heavy weather. But being ill equipped, with only a sail, a bailing bucket, and no navigation lights, this one had fallen victim on this dark night to the sturdily constructed steel freighter *Sonja*.

Natural Repair

The *Jens Juhl* was another freighter counted amongst the yachting fraternity. The vessel was a Baltic trader, constructed by the Ring Andersen Shipyard of Denmark. A gaff rigged ketch of some 90 ft. in length, she was kept original and not, as most, converted to a yacht. Built before the Second World War, the vessel was meticulously maintained by her owner, Kenny, a fellow of dark complexion and gypsy like appearance. His efforts were enthusiastically aided by his wife, two children, Johnny the mate, and a continuous flow of transient young people looking for adventure. One would have to be hard pressed to find a nicer bunch of people and a happier ship than *Jens Juhl*. I always thought that if ever a movie director were in need of a cast for a pirate movie, he could not make a better pick than by choosing Kenny, his ship, and his motley crew.

Kenny came to face an incident which neither made a great impact on their operation nor was it of any significant importance, but it made me remember a story I once read about a clipper ship which had difficulty in prying loose a crate containing cargo from one of its holds. Apparently the ship's hull side had been pierced by a giant sword fish whose bill had penetrated the hull and the crate and then embedded itself into one of the deck beams. Yet, the ship had not leaked noticeably more than usual since where the fish had pierced the hull, the bill had also plugged the hole with a tight fit. The crate was firmly fastened by 'the sword' of this enormously large specimen and it took colossal effort to cut it loose.

Jens Juhl had developed a leak, the origin of which could not be found despite several efforts. Then, it mysteriously stopped. When lying alongside the wharf in Kingstown, St. Vincent, Kenny had discharged the last of the remaining cargo. It was now Johnny's job to inspect the empty hold to ensure that everything was 'ship shape' to receive the new load. As he meticulously inspected every nook and cranny he suddenly came upon an extraordinary sight. The head of a small fish could be seen sticking out from one of the massive timbers to which the hull planking was fastened. He called Kenny and showed him his discovery. Together they looked at this phenomenon and then they carefully removed the dead fish from its coffin. The instant they managed to pull the last bits of fish from the timber, water started pouring into the ship. They promptly plugged the hole with a wooden dowel.

Apparently, the galvanized iron bolt which had previously occupied the hole had snapped and fallen out. This was the mysterious leak they had been unable to find. It had been hidden by the cargo which had just been unloaded. Somehow, a curious fish had come moseying along and had either swam, or, more likely, was sucked into the hole. The fish had provided a water tight seal that had lasted for several days!

Contraband

As soon as we approached the anchorage of Admiralty Bay in Bequia, I spotted the cargo schooner *Fantasy*. Like *Jens Juhl*, she was an unconverted Baltic Trader and plied the Caribbean sea carrying freight. I knew her mate, Charlie, better than her owner who often left the ship for long periods of time, entrusting the operation to Charlie and his crew. I had not seen *Fantasy* and Charlie for some time. I had heard that the ship had been taken to Denmark for a refit. But here she was, back again in her familiar anchorage. And she looked spectacular! Her hull was gleaming with fresh paint and her cap rail and spars, obviously new, sparkled with varnish.

The first person I ran into when I landed on shore was Charlie. He was waiting for me at the dinghy dock.

"Hi Jan, saw you come in. Long time no see!"

"Hello there, Charlie, nice to see you. Where have you been all this time?"

"Let's go to the Frangipani. I'll buy you a beer and tell you all about it."

Settling down in one of the chairs at Bequia's favourite hangout for yachties, Charlie began to tell me his story.

"Did you see *Fantasy* when you came in?"

"Sure did: couldn't miss her. She looks magnificent!"

"I own her now. I bought her and gave her a complete refit in Denmark."

"You bought her? Did you rob a bank?" I asked jokingly.

"Better than that. I bought her, paid for her refit and just deposited a big pile of money into the bank."

Amazed, I looked at him. "You did rob a bank!" I exclaimed. "Or you had a rich aunt who died after robbing one for you!"

"No, none of that." He shook his head and took a sip of his drink. Then, lowering his voice, he said, "I did a job for some people in the States, something like the Mafia."

I stared at him, perplexed. "You didn't knock somebody off did you?" I couldn't suppress a nervous chuckle.

"No, are you kidding, of course not. No, I hauled some dope, hashish. It was as easy as pie. An incredibly well organized deal."

"Jesus, Charlie," I looked around me to see if anyone was listening. "You ought to be careful with what you are saying. You did this with *Fantasy* ?"

He looked at the occupants of the other tables. "It's OK, nobody can hear us. No not with *Fantasy*, are you mad? Of course not, she would have been too conspicuous. No, the boat was all arranged for me. I picked her up in New York. A nice motor yacht. I took her down to Colombia, to a pre-arranged harbour, and there she was loaded up with the stuff. Then they hauled her out and raised the waterline to make it look as if she was lying in the water normally, without additional

The Frangipani

weight. On my way back I was given instructions by radio to take her directly back to New York where I was to be at a certain place, off the coast, at a certain time. When I arrived, there were several boats of a similar type waiting for me. Just hanging around, fishing."

Charlie took another sip of his drink as I listened and watched him, spell bound. He put his glass down, looked around to make certain no one could hear, and continued.

"As soon as I arrived, they all closed in around me and then we went toward the shore and into the harbour. When we arrived in the marina, I was told to take the boat to the lift to be hauled out. The machine was ready and waiting for me. I got off and watched them unload the stuff while some guy repainted the water line. After a while, a taxi pulled up and a fellow came out who told me to get in. He opened the door and pointed to a large suitcase which was full of money. I got in and the taxi drove off, taking me to the airport. Even the flight ticket was supplied and my seat had been reserved. About four hours later I arrived in St. Thomas. Nothing to it! The whole thing went off like a well oiled machine."

I had listened to Charlie's tale with fascination. "From New York all the way to Colombia and back, how did you arrange for fuel for such a long trip?" I asked.

"That was all arranged too," Charlie replied. "On the way down it was easy of course. The boat was empty so I could just stop at various ports to fill up. But on the way back, it was arranged in the same way as my arrival in New York. I would get a call on the radio, with a chat about fishing. Something like, "Hello Charlie, are you having any luck?" I would answer, "No, they aren't biting." Then he would say, "We are in a good spot, lots of fish. Why don't you try your luck here?" That would be my cue that everything was ready. I would go to the designated location, always just before dusk or very early in the morning, and several boats would be fishing in the area. As soon I arrived, they would sort of hang around me, while one of them transferred fuel into my tanks. Like I said, everything was organized to the smallest detail. Those guys are real professionals."

Charlie fell silent as he stared into the distance, his eyes not seeing, his mind picturing and reliving the images of his illegal adventure. I sat quietly, digesting the tale I'd just been told. In my mind, there was no question that the story did not come from Charlie's imagination. The details were accurate, the plot well conceived. The proof was lying at anchor in the harbour. This is how it can be done and obviously, this is how it is done.

Suddenly, Charlie broke the silence. "You know, Jan, I don't want you to think bad of me. After all it was only hash. Hell, there's nothing wrong with the stuff. I smoke it all the time. If it had been cocaine or something like that, I wouldn't have done it."

Why did Charlie confide in me? I don't know. But I had a strong suspicion that he was slightly 'under the influence' while he told me his tale. Possibly he wanted to unburden his soul, or was so excited about his success that he just had to tell someone. Perhaps I just happened to be in the right place at the right time!

For obvious reasons the names, 'Charlie' and '*Fantasy*' are fiction, but the story and the characters are real!

The Piano

Grenada lies along the route of several visiting cruise ships. There is room at the commercial dock inside the harbour of St. George's for the smaller ones, but the large ships often anchor outside and ferry the passengers onshore in their launches. The visit usually lasts for about eight hours. The ships arrive in the morning and depart in the late afternoon.

The presence of a cruise ship somewhat upsets the usual sleepy, daily curriculum of the town of St. George's. Suddenly hundreds, if not thousands, of tourists are deposited along the harbour front. Most wander through the town. Some get into taxis for sightseeing tours, while others board the *Rumrunner,* a catamaran type vessel with a palm frond roof that takes the tourists on a trip to a local reef for snorkeling. The boat has a 'steel band' onboard and the rum punch flows in liberal quantities. The condition of the *Rumrunner's* passengers, after the return of yet another successful trip, is often quite a spectacle to behold.

In Barbados, this Rumrunner type entertainment is provided by the *Jolly Roger*, a local schooner done up like a Pirate ship. At one time her return into the harbour of Bridgetown caused quite a commotion. One of the tourists, a somewhat overweight lady, had managed to climb the rigging, taking off and throwing away her clothes as she ascended to great heights.

"Take me as I am!" she yelled at the top of her voice and with her arms spread wide, as she stood naked on the crows nest of the foremast, in plain view of everyone on shore.

Jules and I happened to be in the vicinity of the cruise ship dock in St. George's when the launches arrived, discharging the passengers from a large ship anchored just outside the harbour. I noticed that the sailors operating the launches wore the insignia of the Holland America Line on their uniforms. I approached one of them and started to chat in my native language. I learned that they were off the *Rotterdam* and that the ship was on her last voyage. The ship was getting old and had been sold to a Japanese company.

"Why don't you and your lady go onboard and take a last look?" the chap offered.

I looked at Jules. "What do you think, shall we?"

"Why not?" she answered. "Let's go for a bit of nostalgia, it'll remind us of the days when you were in the merchant marine."

She hit it right on the nose. Although I had not sailed on liners, but on freighters with passenger accommodation, the feel and workings of these ships was not all that much different. I had sailed on a Holland American Line ship for a short time, the *Dalerdijk*, but she also was mainly a freighter and carried no more than a small amount of passengers. I remembered having been onboard the *Rotterdam* once, while she was in between cruises, many years ago in Holland, and I remembered her to be a beautiful ship of the older, luxury style.

We boarded one of the launches and soon found ourselves onboard, wandering through the ship under guidance of one of the crew. As we entered one of the large dining rooms I spotted a grand piano. This triggered memories, because fancying myself as somewhat of a musician, I had often considered getting a piano onboard *Ring*. In particular, I remembered the pianos on the ships of the Holland America Line, because they were especially built for this company by Playel, a French maker of fine musical instruments. The pianos built for the ships were manufactured in such a way that they could cope with differences in temperature and humidity as it varied in different parts of the world. Any one of these pianos cost a small fortune.

"Are there any more of these onboard?" I asked our guide, pointing to the instrument.

"Yes, several."

"Are they being sold with the ship, or will they be transferred to one of the others?"

"Not as far as I know," he answered, referring to the latter part of my question. "I think everything is included in the sale."

"Where can we find out for sure?" I asked.

"You'll have to ask someone in the purser's office; they'll know exactly what goes and what stays."

In sudden excitement I grabbed Jules by the hand and said, "Let's go talk to the purser."

"Oh, no! What are you up to now? Even if you can get one, how are you going to get it off the ship and onto *Ring Andersen*?"

"I don't know yet," I said, "but let's go to the purser's office anyhow."

With a sigh she followed.

"Hello," I said to the lady who occupied the front office. "Is the purser around?"

"Yes," she answered, "would you like to see him?"

"Yes, please."

"Just one moment, I'll get him for you." She went into an office behind the counter and a moment later a man in uniform with silver stripes came out and approached us.

"Can I help you?" he said, a friendly smile on his face.

I introduced Jules and myself and explained that we were not passengers but local yachties. I also explained what type of business we were in and that we were sad to hear that the *Rotterdam* was on her last voyage. I then asked about the ship's inventory, if was it all included in the sale and did this include the pianos. I expressed my interest and desire for one of the pianos and if, although I realized it was unlikely, on the off chance it was possible to buy one before the ship went to her new owners.

He listened to me patiently. When I mentioned the piano, his friendly face began to peak with interest. Much to my surprise he suddenly interrupted me and said, "As a matter of fact, the list of inventory is quite sketchy, and I do know that we have one piano onboard which is definitely not on the inventory. It's the baby grand which is located in the forward bar."

I could hardly contain my excitement. "What is going to happen to it when the ship changes hands?" I asked.

He shrugged his shoulders, "Nothing, I guess. It'll stay on the ship and go to the new owners. I'm not aware of any other arrangements that have been made. A piano is hardly worth the company's efforts to worry about when the ship changes hands. If you want to buy it, I'm sure that can be arranged."

"How much?" I asked.

"Oh, I don't know, shall we say, five hundred bucks? How does that sound, but you'll have to make arrangements to get it moved off the ship. Go and have a chat with the bosun, maybe he can be of some help. I also have to run this by the chief purser. I can't do it without his go ahead, although I'm certain he won't have any objections. Why don't you see the bosun and in the meantime I'll try and locate the chief purser. He may have gone ashore."

I could hardly believe my good fortune, a baby grand, one of the famous Holland America Line Playels, for five hundred bucks!

Half an hour later we had located the bosun and explained our little transaction. "Sure," he said, "I'd rather see it end up in your hands than in Tokyo. He had fought in the second world war and still regarded the Japanese as enemies. He accompanied us to the forward bar. He took a look at the piano and studied its location. "No problem," he said, we'll move it onto the foredeck and from there lower it over the side with one of the derricks. If you bring your boat alongside and hold her in the proper place, we'll put it on your decks, but you'll have to give us a tune as you sail away," he added with a grin.

"Done," I said, and explained that I had to get back to the purser to make the final arrangements.

"Don't worry," the bosun said, "we'll keep an eye out for your yacht; when you come alongside we'll be ready."

Thanking him, Jules and I rushed back to the purser's office.

"Haven't located him yet," the purser said. "He is off watch and must have gone ashore. I have sent someone to look for him." He looked at his watch. "It's now 12.30 hours, we sail at 16.00. That doesn't give us much time."

"Also," Jules added, "our crew knows nothing about this. We better let them know to stand by."

"Right," I agreed, "why don't you go back to *Ring* and tell the crew to get the yacht ready for sailing. I'll wait here for the chief purser and join you as soon as we've got his okay."

Jules left and I waited. One hour went by and then another. The purser and I looked at our watches. We both shook our heads.

"It's too late," I said, even if he shows up now we can't do it. By the time I get back onboard and move Ring Andersen alongside it will be at least another hour. If you're leaving at 16.00, your captain won't allow the deck crew to fart around with a piano so close to sailing time. They will be needed to prepare for departure."

"You're right," the purser agreed with a sigh. "They won't hold the ship up for this, 16.00 hours is 16.00 hours, not a minute sooner, or later.

Disappointed, we shook hands and I left the ship.

Some hours later, Jules and I were sitting in the salon with me staring at the spot where I had envisioned my baby grand piano, when we heard the radio crackle.

"Ring Andersen, Ring Andersen, this is the Rotterdam."

I picked up the mike and answered, "Go ahead Rotterdam, this is the Ring Andersen."

"If you still want that piano, we can drop it off somewhere for you. We are bound for St. Thomas, we can unload it there."

"When will you be in St. Thomas?"

"Tomorrow afternoon."

"It will take me several days to get there, where will you store the piano?"

"We'll put it on the dock and put a tarp over it..., if they let us."

I thought about that for a minute, envisioning a beautiful grand piano standing on the commercial dock in St. Thomas for several days. Providing it survived the curiosity from local dock workers, it would be exposed to the tropical sun and rain squalls. The instrument wouldn't have a chance.

"Rotterdam, this is the Ring Andersen, I really appreciate the offer, but no, that won't work, I think the piano is better off in Tokyo. You guys have a good trip and next time you're in the neighbourhood, drop by and I'll buy you a beer."

I hung up the mike and went back into the salon and again stared at the spot where the baby grand should have been.

The Deal

Some years ago, before I operated a charter yacht, I met an individual who fixed up old boats and then sold them. You, my valued reader, have met him in the beginning of '*No Shoes Allowed*', the predecessor to this book. This fellow believed that if a boat didn't sell for the asking price, then the best course of action was to raise the price. He believed that a more expensive boat would be easier to sell since the prospective buyer would automatically assume that he was getting a better boat. He proved his theory with a boat he tried to sell to me. At first he asked twelve thousand dollars for it. When no one made him an offer, a couple of weeks later, he increased the price by a few thousand dollars. He did this three times, until eventually, believe it or not, he found a buyer and sold the boat for sixteen thousand dollars! I was reminded of the chap's novel sales technique when Walter Budreau, owner and operator of the yacht *Janine*, developed health problems.

The *Janine* was a beautiful schooner, about the same size as the *Ring Andersen*. Walter kept his yacht in Bristol fashion and offered first class service to his clientele. Walter was a true pro who had been in the charter game for many years, well before I acquired the *Ring Andersen*. Walter contacted me by phone and said that he had a bad back problem. The prognosis was that it would take considerable time to heal. Several charters were booked on his vessel and he didn't think he could honour them. Walter asked if I could take his bookings. We compared schedules and found that I could take care of some but not all of his charters. As a result, Walter sent an explanatory letter to his clients and recommended *Ring Andersen* to those for whom we were available. They all accepted his recommendation except one party that had decided to make other arrangements. As the season approached, the week that I had reserved for them was rebooked by another group. I thought nothing more of it until, six or seven months later, we arrived in Admiralty Bay at the island of Bequia with a charter party on board.

We had arrived in the early afternoon and our guests had gone ashore to see the island. When they came back on board, they told us of their meeting with charter guests from another yacht. Those people had asked my group questions about the *Ring Andersen*. The reason for their inquiries was that they were the ones who were originally booked on *Janine* and had decided not to accept Walter Budreau's recommendation. The reason was the price. The yacht they had chartered instead was more expensive! They therefore assumed that it was better. However, when they saw *Ring Andersen* arriving in the anchorage earlier that day, they were not so certain anymore.

Having spotted our guests going ashore and deciding to investigate, they confronted our group while entering the Frangipani Hotel for refreshments. My guests, taking pride in *Ring*, promptly asked them over for after dinner cocktails, providing that was okay with the Captain. I had no objection, in fact was looking forward to it, and confirmed the event to the other yacht by radio. After dinner, I sent a boat over to collect them. That evening, when I met them, I learned that indeed they had made their selection based on the charter fee. We had lost out because our fee was two thousand dollars per week less than that charged by the other boat. The yacht they had taken was new in the area and unknown to us. It soon became obvious that they were not happy with their decision and would have rather been on *Ring*.

As of that moment I regularly scrutinized the charter fees of the other yachts and as soon as someone else's rates went up, ours went up too, and higher! I guess for those to whom money is no object, more expensive means better! But there is always an exception to the rule.

Harry, who was a self made man and a millionaire many times over, was one of our favourite repeat customers. He and his wife, accompanied by another couple, chartered with us, often several times in the same season, and always for a minimum of two weeks. Harry was a compulsive bargain hunter, always looking for a deal! Harry was well into his seventies and he enjoyed all the good things in life. A regular traveller - safaris, polar expeditions, jungle trips - Harry was game for everything and always on the move. Very healthy and full of zest, with his wife in tow, he was always ready for a new adventure. When at one time we were climbing the slopes of the volcano in St. Lucia, Harry and I in front and the others falling back behind, he stopped, turned, and yelled at his much younger wife, "Come on and hurry up, you slow poke, otherwise I'll have to trade you for a younger one. I have done it before, so hurry!"

As I said, Harry was a bargain hunter and always after a deal. This was driven to the extreme when he and his friends invited Jules to come with them for a trip to Point a Pitre, the capital of Guadeloupe. We were anchored in Des Hayes, a bay at the north western end of the island. The trip to Point a Pitre required automotive transportation. Two taxis were ordered, Harry didn't like being crowded, and the group of five took off for the city. While in the shopping district, Harry started looking for Betty, his wife, who had wondered off to one of the shops. He found her in a store selling leather goods. Betty was just about to purchase a purse when Harry stopped her.

"Wait a minute, how much is this purse?"

"One hundred and eighty francs, why?"

"Let me see if I can make a better deal." Turning to the shop keeper, Harry said, "How much for two purses?"

The man scratched his head, made some calculations on a piece of paper and answered,

"Three hundred and thirty francs."

"Ha, you see!" said Harry to his wife, "that's a discount of thirty francs. Just you wait." He turned back to the shopkeeper and said, "Okay, one for one hundred and eighty, two for three hundred and thirty, so how much would you charge for four purses?" He looked at the man expectantly.

"But, Harry..." his wife began.

"Hush, my dear," Harry interrupted, "let the man figure it out. I think we can make a real deal here."

The shopkeeper looked up from his note pad and said,

Anchored in the Tobago Keys

Ring *off the coast of Grenada*

In the Grenadines.
PSV and her beaches

Coming in to anchorage

"Six hundred and thirty francs."

"Right," said Harry, "I'll take all four of them." and he pulled out his wallet. Triumphantly he looked at his wife, "See, that's how you make a deal, I've got those purses now for ninety francs less than you would have paid."

"But Harry, I don't want four purses, I only want one."

"Never mind that, you take one, we'll give one to Jules, one for Jane and the other one, well, we'll think of someone." With this he picked up the parcel containing the purses and marched out of the door. Passing the package to the taxi driver who had been waiting outside, he said, "Here put this in the trunk, there's more to come." He grabbed Betty's hand and said, pulling her along, "Come dear, let's go to the next shop and see if we can make more deals."

I had become used to Harry's ways of doing business. He would phone me from his home in Florida and say, "Hello, Jan, we were just talking about the *Ring* and thought that we might want to go for another trip. What kind of deal can you make us?"

"Well, gee, Harry, for you, of course I'll give you a good deal. Let me see," I'd wait a few minutes pretending I was doing a lot of calculating, and then I would say, "Harry, we have just increased our rates, but for you it'll be the old rates and I'll tell you what, Harry, I'll throw in the booze for free. How's that?" I could easily make that offer, because Harry didn't even know what our rates were and the little bit of liquor they consumed I never charged them for anyway.

"Wow, Jan, that's one hell of a deal. Okay, we're coming down."

Regardless of Harry's insistence on making deals, he was a very generous man and always left a good tip for the crew. At one time, when I found myself in a tight spot because of a major equipment breakdown, Harry and his friend Ed came immediately to my assistance with a loan. Thanks to them, I was able to make the costly repairs in time to meet our charter schedule. Unfortunately, we have lost touch and I haven't seen them for a long time, but I can picture Harry in some far away land, bargaining for a local treasure with Betty at his side.

Technical Stuff and Hamburgers

The yacht *Elisa* had come back from an extensive refit carried out at a well known yard in Europe. She had been gone over with a fine tooth-comb and was now back in Grenada, and she was being hauled out for bottom painting. Since the refit the owners had been running into a re-occurring problem: no sooner had the bottom been painted and the boat launched, then a few days later they found large sections of the paint had peeled away. This had never been a problem before the refit and nobody could understand what caused it. The owners were quite concerned because the exercise of hauling and bottom painting is an expensive procedure. Phone calls were made to the European shipyard to find out what they had done that could cause this problem. No satisfactory solution was found and eventually the owner started submitting claims to Lloyds, the insurers. This resulted in an invasion of adjusters, engineers and surveyors from all points of the globe descending on the boat to probe, inspect, reason, argue, in an attempt to find the rationale for this extraordinary phenomenon.

However, none could pinpoint the problem. Desperate for answers the Lloyds representative from Trinidad asked if I would give it a go. He knew I had done surveys in the past and he knew that I had an extensive background in the marine industry. What really encouraged him to approach me was the fact that I had grown up in the ship building environment due to my grandfather's boat yard in Holland. Every male member in the family either worked in the yard or ended up going to sea. I had done both. As a child, the yard was my playground, the yard workers always offering me advice or lending me a helping hand when building anything that would float. Holidays from Merchant Naval Academy were spent working in the yard to help pay the tuition fees. Although I didn't think that I would be able to do any better where all the other experts had failed, I accepted the assignment.

The problem with the boat had already been widely discussed amongst the yachting fraternity in the marina. Everyone agreed that it had to be an electrical problem. The yacht was built of steel. Antifouling bottom paints as a rule contain copper which deters marine growth. The reaction between the two metals, steel and copper, caused by electrolysis can cause damage to the steel. The combination of steel and copper submerged in salt water works similar to a battery, setting up an electric current. I won't go into all the boring details of what precautions can be taken to avoid this electrolytic action. All the normal procedures to forego this problem had been taken, examined and re-examined. In that regard, everything was as it should be.

What then was the problem? I did all the things the

other investigators had probably already done. I checked the barrier coat, the zinc anodes and the electrical circuitry. I spent considerable time in the battery compartment but found nothing out of whack there. The yacht had been completely rewired and the job appeared to have been carried out with great diligence and expertise. I spent the better part of the day going through the yacht's systems but found nothing out of the ordinary. About to give up and wondering how to relate the bad news to the Lloyds man from Trinidad, I sat in the yacht's luxuriously appointed salon admiring the beautiful joinery and attractive fixtures. Then, suddenly, and I still don't know what made me do it, perhaps it was the spirit of my long dead grandfather, I decided to remove one of the light fixtures mounted against the sides of the salon. I took a screw driver and removed one of them from its base. The unit was fastened onto the teak paneling but there was an electrical connection between the base and the steel frame of the deckhouse. When I disassembled the fixture and examined the wiring, I noticed to my surprise that only one wire came up from behind the paneling: one instead of two, one positive and one negative. I picked up my volt meter and connected a lead to the wire, the other one to the metal of the hull, then I pressed the switch of the light fixture and bingo, contact was made. I put down the fixture, screwdriver, and voltmeter and rushed back to the battery compartment. The main battery leads disappeared through an opening in a bulkhead. I followed the leads by removing drawers from a counter and there, there was the answer, the negative wire from the batteries was bolted to a frame in the hull. The yacht was wired like a car! The body, the hull, was the negative. Not a good idea for a boat. A car sits on rubber tires and is insulated from the ground. Not so with a boat, it makes direct contact with the water. Every time a switch is turned on, a surge of electrical current goes through the hull, causing major electrolysis.

I ran to the phone and called Trinidad. I explained what I had found and suggested they call the yard in Europe and demand an explanation. The next day I was told that apparently the electrician who had rewired the boat had been newly hired by the yard and had come with excellent references. He had a long, very satisfactory employment record with Mercedes Benz in Stuttgart!

And this brings me to hamburgers. When one of our charter guests decided he wanted to buy his own yacht, having heard of my impressive victory even though it was accomplished through pure luck, he asked me to survey his intended purchase.

Richard Walker was an extremely wealthy man who owned a chain of supermarkets and other well prosperous businesses. He had chartered *Ring* several times and usually came with his wife and two friends. I knew Richard well enough to know that he was of the old guard: very conservative and prudent in his business dealings. Everything he owned was his; no finance companies, no mortgages. He was in his seventies and still actively engaged in his business empire. Although he had always been extremely generous as a charter guest, when it came to business he would go to great lengths to save a nickel here or there. I had spent some time with him and his charming wife Alice at his home in Newport, Rhode Island. He asked me to come and see him to look over some boat plans and paid for my flight, expenses and a handsome consulting fee. This is the other side of Richard: he doesn't mind spending money on a sudden whim. To this day I don't know why he wanted me to see the plans. I don't think he had any intention of having the boat built. We spent at most an hour looking at the plans and then started driving around calling in at various car lots where they sold recreational vehicles. He explained to me that he was looking for a camper, the type that is mounted onto the back of a pickup truck. Not for him but for his accountant. He felt the man spent too much money staying in hotels while making the rounds to audit the various supermarkets. All of the stores had parking lots and it would be much more economical if the accountant could conduct his business from his compact mobile unit while at the same time having accommodation for the night. The man would now be able to cook his own meals too; another saving. At first I thought Richard was kidding, but no, he was dead serious.

Several months after my visit to Newport, Richard became a widower. We exchanged telephone calls and letters and then, except for the occasional post card, lost touch. About a year later when we arrived in Grenada with a charter party onboard, a message was left with the office to call him urgently. When I spoke with him he explained that the sudden death of Alice had prompted him to change his lifestyle. He had sold his super markets for many millions of dollars. Now he had more free time on his hands. His cruises on *Ring Andersen* had whetted his appetite; he wanted to go sailing and buy his own yacht. The boat he was interested in was lying in Majorca in the Mediterranean and was for sale for just under sixteen million dollars. The boat had been built in Holland and was only a few years old. Richard asked me to join him in Newport; from there we would fly together to Spain and then on to Majorca.

Richard and I arrived in Madrid where we were to change planes for the flight to Majorca. It was a two hour wait for the connecting flight which allowed us to stretch our legs and do some sightseeing in the close vicinity of the airport terminal. When we stepped out of the building Richard uttered an exclamation of delight.

"You see that across the street?"

I looked but didn't spot anything of particular interest.

" Over there," he pointed excitedly, "McDonald's, the Big Mac!"

"Ah, yes, so it is, even here in Spain." But I didn't think the discovery warranted his excitement. "Why? Is this another part of your financial empire?"

"Hell no, I just like hamburgers and theirs are really cheap. That's great because now I know where we'll be eating. If they're here in Madrid, I bet they'll be in Majorca too. Maybe there's a Kentucky Fried as well. Let's go and look."

And low and behold, just around the corner we spotted the Colonel. Richard was in good spirits.

We landed in Majorca in the late afternoon and checked into a hotel operated by the yacht club and located at the marina where the yacht was berthed. It's amazing how transient and small the yachting fraternity is, because although I had never been in Majorca before and didn't expect to find anyone there that I knew, I was soon proved wrong.

After checking in at the hotel and leaving Richard to

settle down and take a nap, I went for a walk to explore the area. Outside the hotel I spotted a small bistro with outside seating. The place was busy with clients. I decided to enter and ordered a coffee. I love Spanish coffee. A little bit of very strong coffee in a small cup topped up with boiling milk, add some sugar and wow, absolute delight! I had no sooner sat down when someone called my name. To my surprise there was one of the Caribbean yachties. In no time flat I was surrounded by four more. All old friends from Grenada. Then more arrived, among them Simon and Nicki Bridger. I had known them for many years, back when Simon was running *Harvey Gamage*, a large topsail schooner. Simon had moved to Majorca and was just in the beginning stages of setting up a yacht management company. That night I was invited for dinner at Simon and Nicki's house. That got me out of a meal at McDonald's with Richard.

The next day I started the survey on the yacht while it was lying in the water. The underwater portion would be carried out later when an appointment was made with the local yard. In the mean time, Richard was in his element because he had tracked down the location of both a McDonald's and a Kentucky Fried Chicken. But another problem had started to develop. The boat was fully crewed and for some reason Richard didn't like the captain. Several times during the ensuing days he would make some disparaging comment about the man. I also found some defects in the rigging. A couple of turnbuckles had cracks in them. However, that problem was quickly solved when I mentioned it to the yacht's owner, the vendor, who had come down for the occasion. The man promptly picked up the phone and made a call to a rigger in England. The next day a team of riggers arrived with replacement parts. They had flown in by private jet, as ordered by the owner. When I asked one of the riggers how much this little repair job cost, he said: "About fifteen thousand pounds, but that includes the cost for the jet." Well I would hope so, fifteen thousand pounds would almost buy the whole of a nice little second hand cruiser for the average yachtie.

When I was finished with the in-the-water part of the survey, we found out that the local yard couldn't haul the boat because of it's size. Telephone calls were made and an appointment was made with a shipyard in Barcelona.

I said goodbye to Simon and Nicki and my other re-discovered friends and Richard and I boarded a plane for Barcelona while the crew took the boat across to the mainland. That night we had dinner at McDonald's.

Barcelona, the port where the Spanish Armada's shipyard is located, where Columbus sailed from, home of the famous architect Gaudi. It is a beautiful city with lots of history; ancient buildings and narrow alleys giving access to a multitude of small squares which in the late afternoon were transformed into busy marketplaces. One market was occupied with stands displaying paintings from local artists. So much talent! I couldn't stay away from the place. Eventually, I could not contain myself and bought four oil paintings with scenes of the local countryside. Near to the hotel is a grand, tree lined and wide avenue which seemingly goes on for miles. The avenue is divided by a grassy boulevard with bushes and trees interspaced with paved areas on which market stalls were erected together with book and newsstands, eateries, and amusement facilities. The avenue is edged with buildings of old world architecture containing shops and a variety of restaurants with splendid outside terraces. Amongst them, a McDonald's and a KFC.

The day after our arrival we decided to go to the shipyard to make sure that everything was ready for the haulout. I noticed a large motor yacht being worked on in the dry dock. When I questioned the yard's manager about which dry dock would be hauling the boat, he pointed to the dock with the motor yacht. He also mentioned that they had run into a few complications with the motor yacht and that it would take some time before they could launch her. "How long before you have her ready to go?" I asked. Richard's boat was expected to arrive the next day. "Could be ten, maybe fourteen days," he answered.

Richard had rented a car. As we were driving back to the hotel I made some mental calculations. Normally my charge for doing a survey is calculated at a certain amount of dollars times the length of the boat, but for work that involves a lot of travelling I charge a daily sum plus travelling expenses. There was about one more day of work for me to do. Adding fourteen unproductive days would not be to Richard's advantage. Reminded by Richard's efforts spent in getting his accountant out of a hotel bed and into a little pickup truck, I thought I better discuss the situation with my client.

"Richard, it's going to take at least ten, probably fourteen days before I can finish the survey."

Richard concentrated on his driving as he wound the car through twists and turns of narrow roads, dodging heavy traffic of speeding cars and fast moving scooters.

"Go ahead," he said, "I'm listening," as he swerved to escape a scooter that cut in front of us.

"Well, the way I see it," I had put one hand on the dash board bracing myself, "we can do one of two things. Either we find a local surveyor and get him to do the rest of the survey, I can make some notes of the things left to do, in which case I fly home tomorrow, or, I stay, in which case it would not be fair for me to charge you my daily fee for the days that I'm not working. But I would expect you to pay for my lodging and other expenses. The most economical thing would be for me to go back tomorrow."

Richard surprised me again. He said, "You know, I have never been to Spain. Actually, I don't know this part of the world at all. We have fourteen days, so why don't we go on a tour and see the countryside? And don't worry about your fee, you've got to earn a living. What do you say?"

I couldn't believe my ears and said hastily, "Sounds good to me, Richard."

Braking hard for a truck that pulled ahead of us from a side road, he said, "Good. That's settled then. Now it's getting close to dinner time. Keep your eyes open for a McDonald's, there should be one around here somewhere." And he added, mumbling, "I hate spending money on fancy restaurants."

On the corner of a street a bit further along, he spotted his favourite hangout and we joined the crowd.

The next day we started our tour. We cruised up along the east coast of Spain, the Costa Bravo. Arenys de Mar, Calella, Palamos, Rosas, quaint villages along the Mediterranean, fishing ports, white washed buildings, sandy beaches, a visit to a pottery factory where I bought a large porcelain bowl with intricate, hand painted design. Overnight stops at nice hotels on the water's edge. Then into France along the Gulf of Lions and on to Cannes, Nice, across another border into Italy, San Remo, and then it was time to turn back. We headed inland and drove back into Spain, winding through the Pyrenees. I was delighted with what we saw, the local architecture, the vistas of the landscape. So was Richard, and as a bonus, yes, the Golden Arches and the Colonel are well represented, even there.

I had finished the survey. The yacht was in good shape. Only one problem left to deal with: the captain. Richard did not want him on his boat. In fact, he wanted to get rid of the entire crew. According to Richard they were all contaminated by the boat's skipper. The situation presented a problem because this survey was also for the insurers which happened to be Lloyds and they wanted a report not only on the boat but also an assessment of the crew. This I think is very wise, because I am of the opinion that a poor boat with a good crew is a better insurance risk than a good boat with a bad crew. Several calls had been made to the Lloyds syndicate and I had recommended that the crew stay on board. The skipper was well experienced, had been on the yacht since she was built, and carried out his job in an efficient manner. The crew also were knowledgeable and the team worked together well. I had observed this as I carried out the survey and, during the sea trial and through perusing their resumes. But no matter how I tried, Richard was adamant: the whole lot had to go. He knew this guy back home who was a sailing instructor and he wanted him to be the captain. As far as the rest of the crew was concerned, the fellow back home would be able to hussle up some of his sailing buddies.

"But Richard, I hope that isn't his only claim to fame. You must understand that although the man may be a sailing instructor, there is a big difference between a guy who teaches sailing in local waters on a small boat, and the person capable of running a yacht of this size on the open ocean going to foreign ports." Richard wanted the boat to go to the Caribbean and then to the South Pacific.

Again Richard was on the phone to the man from Lloyds. I overheard the conversation. It was about the crew; the captain and his man from back home. Eventually some agreement was reached. I heard Richard say, "I'll ask him."

He turned to me and said, "He wants to talk to you," and handed me the phone.

"Hello?"

"OK, here is my suggestion. Can you take the boat to the Caribbean? That will be agreeable to the underwriters and when the boat gets there you either stay on, or otherwise, by that time hopefully another suitable arrangement can be made."

I thought about it a minute and said, "I will let you know tomorrow, there are a few things I have to sort out, okay?"

"That's fine, but I hope you can do it. It would be a perfect solution."

We said goodbye and I put the phone back in it's cradle.

"Well?" said Richard.

"Offhand that sounds good," I replied, "but it will depend on the time schedule. I'll have to make some calls.

We have charters coming up and I don't know the exact date that I have to be back in Grenada. I have been gone much longer than originally expected already." I looked at my watch. "It's too early now. Allowing for the time difference they won't be up for another couple of hours. I'll have to call Grenada later."

It wasn't until late afternoon when I finally made contact with Jules who was looking after things on *Ring Andersen*. I brought her up to date on the latest state of affairs. Apparently, *Ring* had to be ready for charter in twenty six days. I figured that if everything went smoothly I could make the crossing in about sixteen to eighteen days. Add on a few days to get the boat ready for the trip (we had to get a crew, provisions, and so on). There wasn't much leeway, but it looked like it could be done if there were no complications. I got out my notepad and pen and started to jot down things that pertained to the forthcoming voyage. We'd probably make a stop in Gibraltar to top up fuel and water, than another stop in the Canary Islands. Yes, it was a tight squeeze all right. I spent several hours going over my notes.

Richard knocked on the door of my hotel room.

"It's time to go for dinner."

I looked at my watch. "Oh wow, it's eight o'clock already. Had no idea it was that late."

"Have you been bent over those papers all this time? I had a nap and I'm hungry. Let's go."

We walked out of the hotel into a beautiful and pleasant summer evening. The heat of the day had settled down, promising a comfortable walk.

Barcelona comes alive at night. The place closes down for siesta time between noon and three o'clock when one could rattle off a machine gun through the deserted streets without doing any harm. Evenings are a different thing all together. The streets are crowded with people dressed up in their best duds, out for a stroll, visiting the market stalls, looking for their favourite restaurant, out for an evening's entertainment. We soon found ourselves mingling with the crowd on the main avenue, heading into the direction of, that's right, McDonald's, when Richard suddenly said,

"This could be one of our last nights in Barcelona, maybe we should eat in one of the local restaurants: sample the local food."

Just then we were about to pass an establishment that was a beehive of activity. Tables and chairs arranged on an outside terrace could be seen to continue deep within the building of which the entire front was open. Every chair appeared to be occupied, cheerfully coloured cloths on the tables, bottles of wine, plates laden with food, waiters rushing about.

I looked at Richard and said, "I think you just came up with an excellent idea and it looks like this might be the place."

"You think so?" he said. "But it doesn't look like there is any room."

He had no sooner finished his sentence when a tall and lanky maitre d' with shiny, slicked back black hair and dressed in a tuxedo rushed out of the restaurant toward us. In good English he said,

"Are you gentlemen joining us for dinner?"

Richard's face cheered up hearing the familiar language which put him comfortably at ease in this foreign land.

"Yes," he answered with authority, "A table for two

please."

"As you wish sir," the man replied smoothly as he bowed and waved his arm directing us inside. After a few steps through the crowded place he slid past us with long strides and said, "Please allow me," and gestured us to follow him.

I think the guy was a real pro and recognized a couple of gullible tourists when he saw them. Butter wouldn't melt in his mouth. Bowing and parading in front of us, he led the way into the inner sanctions of the restaurant, then up a long stairway onto a level above the place we had seen from the street. This was no ordinary local eatery, it was a fancy, poshly decorated and obviously expensive eating establishment. I cast a quick eye along the clientele seated at the tables: the men in formal attire, the ladies lavishly outfitted with expensive looking gowns and lots of jewelry, quiet conversation, soft music filtering through from the PA system.

Richard noticed none of this. He was in deep conversation with the guy who had shanghaied us. The gent directed us to a table by the window overlooking the avenue. He pulled back our chairs, getting us seated. Then he stood by the table bending his tall frame, wringing his hands.

"Now, may I make a suggestion?" Not waiting for an answer, he rattled off a number of specialities of the house while at the same time producing two menus which miraculously appeared from thin air. He excused himself and we started perusing the menu. Everything was in Spanish and neither Richard nor I could make head nor tail of it. The specialities which he had recommended had not registered either. After some time went by, the man appeared at our table again. He almost doubled over as he bowed again. He asked us where we were from. When Richard mentioned Newport, Rhode Island, the man professed to know the area intimately which inspired a conspiratory bond with Richard, the maitre d's newly found 'American friend' from Newport. Richard became putty in his hands.

"First time in Spain you say? Ah, you must be unfamiliar with our dishes. Why don't you let me make the selection for you. Leave everything in my hands. I will personally see to it that you are not disappointed. After all, nothing is too good for my American friends from Newport."

I guess he assumed that I was one of Richard's neighbours. But he seemed to instinctively know that Richard was the one he had to please. He busily started to re-arrange the cutlery and dishes on the table. His tall frame bent over our table, his back horizontal and his bum into the air, he turned his head sideways to Richard and said,

"What would you like to drink?" Then he corrected himself, "No, no, leave that to me. I will select the wines for you, we'll start with a fine champagne, then an aperitif. Before we could answer he was off.

"Well," said Richard, "we seem to have found the right place."

The champagne arrived, the cork popped with elegant flourish, the glasses filled, then the entree, the wine, more dishes with delicacies, a different wine, the main course, wine glasses filled promptly, the man hovering around us, but discretely so, always there when needed; desert, coffee, cognac. And then the bill.

Richard picked it up, looked at it, put it down, put on his glasses and looked at it again. He pulled a calculator out of his pocked and converted the currency.

"Eight hundred and forty four dollars," he blurted out. He looked at me with an astonished face, hyperventilating. I thought of smelling salts, artificial respiration, paramedics maybe. Pulling a tissue from his pocket and wiping his forehead he stammered,

"Eight hundred and forty dollars! Even with Alice, rest her soul, I've never spent more than fifty dollars on a meal." Once more he picked up the bill which he had thrown on the table and again studied it. After a moment of hesitation he suddenly said, "Oh, what the hell. Let's face it, the service was excellent and the food delicious. You only live once!" He opened his wallet, counted out the sum of money, and added a handsome tip.

The next morning I gathered my notes and sat down with Richard to discuss the sail to the Caribbean. I thought it prudent to get a few things settled with him before I committed myself and phoned the insurance man in London.

"We have to organize a crew." I said to Richard. "I want to keep the engineer."

"Keep the engineer? Why? I want to get rid of the whole lot."

"Yes, I realize that, but we need him. He has been on the boat for a long time and he knows all the systems. If we bring in a new guy that will delay our trip and we'll be asking for trouble because it will take some time before he is familiar with the boat. Every boat has its own ideosyncrasies and it takes time to get to know them and sometimes at great expense."

Reluctantly, Richard agreed.

"Also, we need at least two capable deck hands and a cook."

This time Richard blew his top, "A cook? What do you need a cook for?"

"To look after the provisioning and to cook the meals consumed on board."

"Can't everybody look after their own meals, sort of pitch in? I don't like cooks. They go out and buy all kinds of expensive stuff, steaks and exotic cheeses from fancy shops. They should be buying bulk, much cheaper. Believe me I know the grocery business."

"Richard, the crew will have their hands full, and so will I, running the boat. I don't want to have to worry about going over the menu and getting the necessary stores on board. Neither the crew nor I will have the time to cook. We'll be running a tight watch system and need sleep and rest when off duty. With the four of us running the boat over that distance we will be short handed as it is."

"Well, I can get a crew together, I'm sure my brother-in-law would like to come and also that sailing instructor I was telling you about. And as far as the cook is concerned, I'll come too and I'll do the cooking."

I thought about what he had said and began to realize that this wasn't going to work out. So far Richard and I had become good friends. I wanted to keep it that way. This trip spelled trouble and I could envision all sorts of unhappy moments arising during an expedition with Richard, his brother-in-law and, the sailing instructor for crew. This was a big yacht and the voyage not just a Sunday afternoon outing. I preferred to keep it on a professional basis with an able crew I could depend on and who would carry out orders when things went wrong. They always do at some point in time. I needed seamen, sailors, not people who just knew how to sail. I also needed an excuse to get out of this situation without offending Richard.

In the early afternoon I called the man from Lloyds. I told him that a decision had not yet been made but that most likely I would not be delivering the boat to the Caribbean.

"So we're back to square one? We can't insure the boat without having a competent captain and crew. So, what do you propose?"

"Leave that to me," I said. "He'll have to let the old crew take the boat, I think they all want to go to Antigua anyhow. Richard can get another crew when the boat gets there."

"Okay, keep me posted."

"Will do." I hung up the phone.

There was a knock on the door. Richard came in. "I have to go to the airport. Want to come along?"

"To the airport? Why?"

"To pick up the sailing instructor. I phoned him yesterday. Told him to get on a plane. He'll be arriving shortly."

This was news to me. Why hadn't he told me? The sneaky bugger. Oh well, it's his boat.

"Oh, I see. No, you go ahead. I'll see you when you get back."

Fifteen minutes after Richard left the phone rang. It was Jules.

"Jan, you can't go on that boat. We've booked another

charter; it starts in ten days."

"Wow, your timing is perfect. That's great news. It'll get me of the hook." I brought Jules up to date on the situation and told her that I would be back home the next day, assuming I could get a flight organized.

Richard arrived with his passenger who turned out to be a very likable fellow. That evening we ate at KFC and while chewing the tender bits, the chap told us that he had made some calculations which told him that the trip to the Caribbean would take ten days. When I asked him how he figured that, he answered that he had measured the distance and divided that by the boat's speed. Upon further questioning he explained that he got his measurements from the in-flight-magazine onboard the aircraft. It displayed the routes the airline flies. He admitted that his estimates were approximate. When I explained to him that the route to the West Indies was not a straight line but diverted via the Canary Islands because of currents and prevailing wind patterns, he frowned his forehead and nodded with appreciative concern.

On the way back to the hotel we stopped at one of the bistros along the Avenue, and while sipping a delicious cup of Spanish coffee I told Richard and the new arrival of Jules' call and the forthcoming charter. I managed to convince Richard that under the circumstances he had no choice but to let the existing captain and crew deliver the boat to the West Indies. I also pointed out that this would be a great opportunity for the sailing instructor to familiarize himself with the operation of the yacht. Perhaps after the trip he would be able to take over as Captain.

The next day I was back on *Ring Andersen*. Several months later I called Richard in Newport and I was told that he was away, cruising in his yacht. His secretary, who had answered the call, said that her boss was having the time of his life but she didn't know who was in charge of running the boat. (I wonder if the slick maitre d' from Barcelona was hired as the cook.)

Stanley's Dilemma

A jump-up is the West Indian version of a party. The event is usually accompanied by a steel band playing reggae, spooch, samba and other lively beats. The rhythm of this music and the resulting acrobatics performed by the dancing crowd will make one understand why this cheerful type of gathering is very appropriately named a 'jump-up'. (Although, toward the end of the evening, the participants having been encouraged by a generous flow of rum punch, the name 'lie-down', sometimes comes to mind.)

Jump-ups are held at regular times at various establishments throughout the Caribbean. If one plans the trip right (or wrong, depending on one's constitution), it is not impossible to hit a jump-up every night at every anchorage encountered along the way. Most charter guests enjoy these outings and for the crews of the charter yachts it is a great opportunity to mix and mingle and to be brought up to date on the local gossip.

We were at the Wednesday night jump-up held at the Mariners Inn in St. Vincent when I spotted Stanley and Elsa of the yacht *Carina* sitting at a table. Their charter guests were on the dance floor. I went over to say hello.

Stanley motioned me to a chair. He looked a bit forlorn.

Stanley and Elsa had done a considerable amount of cruising in their yacht and were looking to chartering mainly because they enjoyed sailing with interesting company. Some of my readers might raise their eyebrows at this last remark, so let me qualify. Chartering is not to be confused with day cruises, booze cruises, or afternoon jaunts around the bay. A charter lasts as a rule for a minimum of one week. The yacht is chartered to one person with his or her close friends or family. Charter groups are rarely larger than six persons. The difference is in the type of people. The members of the group or family that charters a yacht are not usually interested in drinking themselves silly or making a nuisance of themselves. They are on their holidays and want to explore, see and enjoy. They are usually the types who have done many other interesting things, they have travelled a lot, seen a lot.

Without chartering, one could end up with an overdose of Island Fever. (In yachting circles this is sometimes referred to as 'Dock Rot'.) Many cruising yachties have been lured to the islands and stayed too long. Their globe circling ambitions having been side-tracked by a life of leisure and vast quantities of inexpensive liquor. All too many of those cruisers who have enthusiastically planned and budgeted for a long voyage in order to escape the rat race have fallen into the trap of coming to the islands and stayed! Many end up living their everyday existence in the various patio bars throughout the islands. Soon, they lose all motivation and more often than not, with their budget depleted, their boats remain anchored or tied to some dock permanently, usually in poorly

We are transporting the band to the jump-up

maintained condition.

In all my years of chartering I have nothing but good memories of charter guests. Several have ended up becoming life long friends. Most I have found extremely interesting to talk with, and almost all of them I have found to be considerate of my boat, my crew, and myself. In any event, had it not been for chartering, my ship would have had no destination, I would have had no purpose and the lack of income would have caused both of us to suffer from poor maintenance.

Chartering is a healthy compromise between being a member of the corporate machine and the aimless life of a drifter. People who operate charter yachts for a living, take their jobs seriously. It takes a lot of skill to successfully operate a charter business. Besides the obvious requirement of being an excellent seaman, one has to be an efficient business manager, a good host, a respected employer, and a first rate handyman in keeping the equipment in top notch condition.

Since charter yachts operate in remote areas, often the charter skipper has to be resourceful and imaginative. It is very likely that parts or professional expertise are not available when needed. In other words, one has to be a Jack-of-all-trades.

Equal credit must go to the crew of the yacht. Many times I have met young people who assumed that crewing on a charter yacht meant lazing around in the land of fun and sun. I always found it amusing when a job seeker emphasized the fact that he or she knew how to sail or alleged to be rated highly amongst the home-port racing team. The last thing the skipper of a charter yacht is looking for is a person who knows how to sail. What is needed is a person who knows how to work! Scrub, scrape, paint, varnish, polish, carry provisions, etc.

More important than knowing how to sail, is knowing when to be in the right place at the right time, how to put a line on a cleat, how to tie a knot securely and quickly, and how to stop off a line when the yacht comes alongside. There are many who know how to sail, but very few are seamen.

I won't even go into the cooking aspect of chartering because a whole book could be written on that subject. Just think of a yacht's galley: one tenth the size of a kitchen in most homes and slanted at an angle and pitching or rolling. Noise above your head from the clattering of the gear, a stove on which the pots threaten to spill all their contents at the next lurch of the ship. Try turning out a gourmet dinner with all the trimmings for six guests plus crew under those conditions! The galley slaves have my healthy respect!

Obviously, a yachtie working charters is not an amateur but a highly dedicated professional, be they skipper or crew. I am sad to admit that there is the odd yacht to which the term 'professional' only loosely applies. Fortunately they are few and far between. They are disliked by sincere operators and rejected by reputable charter brokers and agents. They give the business a bad name, and most likely have to solicit business direct, since the charter yacht brokers won't deal with them. Usually, this type of operator can be recognized by the state of maintenance of his craft. He more than likely shows as little respect for his boat as he does for his charter guests. A well run charter yacht is kept in Bristol fashion and immaculately clean.

One such yacht was *Carina*, which brings us back to Stanley and Elsa. When I sat down in the chair beside them I learned the reason for the unhappy expression on Stanley's face.

The couple had booked a three week charter to a party of four. They pointed them out on the dance floor. They were very nice people and got along famously with *Carina's* master and mate. There was, however, one problem! One of the male charter guests had become so interested in chatting with Stanley that he followed him everywhere and wouldn't give him a moment's peace. To Stan, who is basically a very private person, and who chartered mainly because Elsa enjoyed it so much, this became a bit of a problem. Realizing the length of the charter, and so far having gone for only ten days, Stanley had become alarmed at the prospect of not having a moment to himself for another eleven days. One night, just before turning in, he had explained his predicament to Elsa.

"You see dear, the man follows me wherever I go, always talking, always asking questions. He is a nice man but I have no privacy at all. Every morning, as soon as I arrive on deck, there he is, waiting for me."

Elsa thought about this for a moment and then came up with an excellent idea.

"Stanley, I'll tell you what we'll do. Tomorrow morning, as soon as you wake up, go quietly up onto the deck through the forward hatch. Stay there by the bowsprit, and as soon as I can, I'll pass you a cup of coffee through the hatch. That way you'll be able to start the day in solitude and enjoy the early morning by yourself."

Stanley thought this was a wonderful solution. Looking forward to a morning with just himself, the rising sun, and the calm waters around him while sipping a steaming hot cup of coffee, he fell into a peaceful sleep that night.

As planned, early the next morning, Stanley crept out of the forward hatch and sat himself down by the bowsprit. A few minutes later, the hatch opened and a cup of coffee was passed through. Stanley closed his eyes in delight as he took the first sip. Suddenly, a voice boomed behind him.

"Good morning, Stanley!"

The cup almost dropped from Stanley's hand. He was too much taken aback to reply. Stanley's favourite charter guest looked down at him with a happy face and continued in a conspiratory manner,

"I can tell you are a man who likes to be by himself once in a while."

Momentarily Stanley's face lit up. The friendly voice continued,

"Well, so am I, you don't mind if I join you, do you?"

Without waiting for a reply, the man seated himself next to his victim and carried on,

"Now, Stanley, tell me, why do you..."

Just then a couple, dancing to the beat of the pans, passed by our table. The man waved to us. "How are you doing, Stanley? This dance is almost over, stay there, I'll come and join you in a minute."

"See what I mean?" said Stanley. "I can't escape him, not even here!"

Wood, Barnacles and Other Stuff

Maintaining a wooden yacht is becoming more and more difficult as time goes on. Fibreglass has practically taken over as a construction material. Steel and aluminum boats are still being built, but fibreglass allows the building of production boats en masse. The same model can be built repeatedly in a relatively economical way by using a form, a mold into which the new hull is laid up. Compared to wood, fibreglass is almost maintenance free, strong, and waterproof. This has forced most of the ship yards who built wooden vessels to switch to fibreglass construction. The majority of those who didn't follow suit closed down voluntarily or went bankrupt. The result is that the profession of shipwright, the carpenter who specializes in the building of wooden boats, has become nearly extinct. This is not yet a problem in the West Indies. I'm saying not yet, because no doubt things will change here too. The building of wooden boats is an art which, to this day, is still practiced in the West Indies. Islands such as Cariacou, Petit Martinique and Bequia are known for the turning out of beautiful fishing boats and large wooden schooners. I have been present at the launching of many a vessel in these islands. These boats are built without architectural drawings or engineering plans. The general design is similar throughout the islands with individual characteristics compliments of the builder, whose knowledge was handed down to him by generations of ancestors, and before that by the whalers from Scotland who frequented these waters regularly. The boat is built with the builder's gut feeling of distinguishing what's right and wrong, and mainly through line of sight and arbitrary measurements.

Mostly hand tools are being used. In fact, when I had shipwrights working on *Ring*, and at one time naively supplied them with power tools, I soon learned that the equipment's chance of survival to the end of the day was hazardous at best.

One of my favourite Grenadian shipwrights was a fellow known as Doc, a small and fragile looking man with the typical friendly and polite West Indian disposition. I guessed him to be somewhere in his late sixties. To give an example of his amazing talent as a shipwright, an introduction to the yacht *Alianora* is in order.

The skipper of *Alianora*, Mike Tate, was not satisfied with the condition of the yacht's teak decks. The yacht was getting on in age and the decks, after many years of scrubbing, had started to wear and were uneven in appearance. Skipper Mike decided to take the boat to Fort Lauderdale where he engaged one of the better known boat yards to overhaul and even-out the deck surface. After many days of planing and sanding with sophisticated machinery, Mike was handed a healthy bill

Ring *hauled out*

Jules touches up Ring's *nameplate*

Local schooners awaiting freight

The framework of a local schooner is almost ready

and told that the job was completed. The finished product had not come close to meeting with Mike's critical expectation, but he was told by the yard that it was impossible to improve on the job they had done. Mike brought the boat back to Grenada where someone suggested he put Doc to work on the problem. Doc arrived on board with his adze, a tool which bears some similarity to a long handled ax, except that the blade is perpendicular to the handle. Doc cast is eyes over *Alianora's* expansive decks and started to chop at the surface near the bow. Several days later, when he had worked his way to the stern, the decks were as smooth and even as a sheet of polished marble.

Doc displayed some of his artistry to me as well. Two of *Ring Andersen's* bullwark stanchions were showing signs of wear and needed to be replaced. Stanchions are like the posts of a fence. They measured six by eight inches in width and extended to twenty nine inches above deck level. At the bottom they entered through the decks through a timber which is called the covering board, and were then sistered (fastened) to the sides of the frames of the hull. The total length of each stanchion was about six feet. At the lower end, each stanchion was slightly curved to meet with the contour of the hull. On the corners, above decks, they had a grooved design that was carved into the wood for decorative purposes. Besides the difficulty of replicating the stanchions to exact shape and design, there was the problem of finding a chunk of wood large enough for the purpose. I discussed the problem with Doc who, after studying the project, nodded his head and said,

"Dat be no problem, Skip. I know a tree up in de hills

dat we can use." He extended his arm, pointing vaguely into the general direction: somewhere inland, east of St. George's.

"What kind of tree?" I asked.

"Local cedar, Skip. Dat real good wood for dis."

"Hum, local cedar hey? Yes, I've heard of that. Isn't that what they use for the frames of the local schooners?"

"Yes Skip."

"Well, good, let's go and get it then."

Doc shook his head, "No, Skip, not yet."

"Why not?"

"De moon, she not right. We have to wait. De moon she still rising, we wait 'till she weans, den de sap of de tree stop flowing. When de sap flow, de wood she rot."

A few weeks later, a twenty foot tree trunk was deposited on the dock beside *Ring Andersen*. The trunk was well over a foot in diameter. Doc had already removed the old stanchions from the boat. They lay alongside the tree, on the dock. With a hand saw he cut the trunk in half. Then Doc started chopping with his adze, occasionally stepping back to look at his work from a distance, comparing it to the old stanchions alongside. He never used a tape measure or a pencil. Every once in a while he would put his hand on the stanchion to be copied, spreading his fingers over it, and then feeling the timber he was working on. After some six hours of chopping, the first new stanchion lay completed on the dock. With the aid of a knife, a chisel, and a chunk of wood used for a hammer, he went to work to engrave the decorative trim. When he was finished, he picked up the new timber, heaved it onboard and stuck the bottom end into the opening in the covering board. It wouldn't go in! Doc picked up his improvised wooden mallet, gave the stanchion a tap and it miraculously slid down into the opening and into its place. I examined it carefully, below and above decks. It was a perfect fit! The second stanchion was installed in the same fashion.

Even amongst the many competent shipwrights in the West Indies, Doc stood out as a man with extraordinary talents. I have never met anyone, anywhere, with such amazing skill.

Ring Andersen had to be hauled out of the water and have her bottom scrubbed and painted regularly. In the tropics the marine growth is tremendous. In Northern latitudes this ritual is only required once a year, possibly less often. It depends on a number of factors: type of anti-fouling paint, moorage location, water temperature, and the amount of active use. In the tropics it has to be done every six months. *Ring's* bottom was sheathed with copper plating. It is commonly believed that if a boat's bottom is covered with copper plates, painting with anti-fouling paint is not necessary. This, however, is a false perception. While the copper plates protect a wooden vessel from toredo worms, they will not prevent other marine life from attaching itself to the ship. Growth slows the boat down and thus interferes with manoeuvrability and efficiency. Growth can be stopped by applying a special paint. It is, however, only effective for a short period of time. Anti-fouling paint is a relatively new invention and was not available during the Middle Ages and the Renaissance when sailing ships were the only means of trans-oceanic transportation. I believe that this is why so many myths are attributed to an area referred to as the Bermuda Triangle. That area lies nearly at the very end of the route from Europe to the Americas. By the time the old square riggers arrived there, after a long voyage from the ports of Europe, their bottoms were so encrusted with barnacles, mussels and other marine life that they could barely move through the water. Especially when the beginning of the passage had been slow due to unfavourable winds, by the time they arrived at the mysterious Bermuda Triangle, food and water would have been a rare commodity indeed. The sailors, hungry, thirsty, superstitious, and possibly delirious as a result, started to imagine all kinds of strange phenomena, like sea monsters, or other strange apparitions, and ghosts, arising from the deep, unknown waters underneath the ship, stopping the vessel from moving even though a fresh breeze was blowing. A crew in that condition would be cause for the demise of any great vessel. The loss of a ship under those circumstances appeals to the imagination of many a science fiction writer.

The place for *Ring Andersen's* regular haul-out was the dry dock at Grenada Yacht Services. This facility consists of a large and heavily constructed steel and wooden platform situated between two concrete walls. Six large, electrically powered winches are located on the concrete walls, one above each one of the four corners, and two in the middle of the longer sides of the rectangular platform. Steel cables wound on drums driven by the winches and leading to the platform allow the operator to raise or lower the contraption with the push of a button. The dry dock, commonly referred to as the lift, was capable of handling a load of about three hundred and fifty tons.

To haul *Ring*, the platform is lowered, the yacht moved

in between the concrete walls, and the platform raised to just touch the bottom of the keel. Then divers go down underneath the ship to place blocks and supports under the hull and keel to ensure that the boat is properly and evenly supported and to hold her secure and stable. The operation is supervised by Julian Rapier, operations manager of the yard and who also was and still is the Chief Pilot of the Port of Grenada. Each time the divers come up for air, they are questioned on the state of progress by Julian. Only when Julian is satisfied that everything is as it should be, he would push the button and raise the platform a few more inches. Again the divers are sent down for a final inspection. A few adjustments here and a few adjustments there, followed by the OK to continue, and then with all the winches humming, *Ring* would slowly rise out of her element and eventually sit high and dry, well above the surrounding yachts and buildings.

Mr. Gullston, also known as Gully, was the chief shipwright of the yard, the importance of his position evident by the fact that, regardless of the hot tropical sun, he wore a formal, black serge jacket and a black felt homburg hat. The silver chain of his pocket watch swung ceremoniously from a button on his coat to a side pocket where the watch was safely tucked away. Armed with his note pad and fountain pen, this dignified personage would invite me to inspect the hull with him to discuss the work to be carried out, each item being carefully recorded on his note pad as we made the rounds.

Having the boat out of the water was always a nervous undertaking for us. The boat felt insecure and foreign by being high and dry and out of her natural environment.

On one such occasion, Karen, our youngest daughter, forgetting that *Ring* was up in the air, used the toilet and flushed it. Unfortunately, it so happened that at that time Mr. Gullston was giving some advice to one of the shipwrights. He was standing directly underneath the through hull opening that serviced that particular toilet. It was a sorry sight to see Mr. Gullston standing there with the unwanted cargo spilling off the brim of his stately hat. It took a lot of apologizing, a bottle of rum, and a new homburg to appease poor Gully.

During that same haul-out, while the shipwrights were working on the boat, Jules and the girls and I had gone into town to do some shopping. We came back to the boat after five o'clock and the workers had finished for the day. When I descended the stairs into the library, to my horror I noticed that the bilges were flooded. Water had risen well over the floor boards. Not having adjusted to the fact that the boat was hauled out with the bottom some twenty feet above sea level, my immediate reaction was to assume that we had sprung a major leak and were sinking. I raced for the controls of the pumps while wracking my brains were the leak could be. I was about to shout instructions to Jules to lower one of the boats, just in case, when suddenly I realized that we couldn't possibly be sinking because the boat was not in the water. As it turned out, the crew had tried to find the source of a small leak. When they couldn't find it, some bright lad suggested to run some water in the bilge with a hose. That way, perhaps, they could find the leak since the water would be leaking out of the boat. However, when five o'clock and quitting time had come around, everyone had gone home, forgetting to turn off the hose.

Grease and Flotsam

For some mysterious reason, I had picked Thomas to become our engineer. Whatever possessed me when I put him in that position I cannot explain to this day. Thus far, Thomas had served as a very capable sailor. Now he was to also perform engineering duties. His new function immediately earned him the name Steambox, so named because Ring's engine was started with compressed air. It involved the opening and closing of a number of valves. The procedure was accompanied by a series of huffing and puffing and a loud hiss when the big flywheel began its initial momentum.

In addition to being able to start the engine, Thomas' duties included the transfer of fuel into the day tank, intimate knowledge of the activation of a number of bilge pumps and related valves to allow the emptying of the various bilge compartments, general tidiness of the engine and generator compartments, and last but not least the regular greasing of the stuffing box of the propeller shaft.

The stuffing box is a sort of bearing through which the propeller shaft exits the hull. To prevent water from coming into the boat, the area surrounding the shaft is stuffed with a wax impregnated material which acts as a bearing. Lubrication is accomplished by the leakage of a small amount of water. This type of stuffing box is called a water lubricated stuffing box. On larger vessels, however, the unit is a little different in that it needs to be lubricated with grease. Ring's stuffing box required greasing at the aft and forward end. For this purpose, a lubricating system was installed that consisted of a heavily constructed bronze container which held about ten pounds of grease. Think of a jam jar with a top that screws on, except in this case, the top screws inside the jar. As one screws down the top, the grease is pressed through two copper tubes which are installed into the bottom of the jar. One tube leads to the aft end of the stuffing box and the other one to the forward end. In each of the tubes, just under the jar, a valve is installed. By opening one of the valves and subsequently screwing down the lid, grease is pushed through the tube with the open valve into the selected section of the stuffing box. This contraption was installed alongside a bulkhead, about twenty feet away from the stuffing box. The exercise of greasing the stuffing box needed to be carried out once every four hours of motoring. Thomas had been doing this faithfully for at least one year when we left West End, Tortola, where we had stopped to clear customs for entering the British Virgin Islands. Our destination, after the brief stop, was Road Town, only a short distance further along the coast of the island. We had no guests onboard and I had decided not to raise the sails and cover the short trip by using the engine. As we were making our way through Drake's Passage, I managed to notice an unfamiliar sound coming from the vicinity of the stern section of the yacht, a dry and raspy sort of grinding sound. The sound was very faint and not noticed by anyone else onboard. I kept listening and wondering what it could be when suddenly I realized the sound came from the propeller shaft. Thomas was washing down the decks not to far away from me. I called him and asked, "Thomas, when did you last grease the stuffing box?"

"Just a little while ago Skip," he looked at his watch, " it be due again in forty minutes. Why you aks, Skip?"

"Something is grinding down there. Go give it a few more turns, will ya?"

"Sure, Skip." Thomas said agreeably, and disappeared into the engine room.

As Thomas went into the engine room, he started to wonder why I would ask him to do something which was out of sync with the regular routine. *Why*, he thought, *is Skip asking me to do dis. Dis ting, she don't need turning for anoder forty minutes.* And then he thought, *what is dis ting actually for? It was explained to me a long time ago. But, since den, dere's been no reason to tink about it. All I has to do is, open de valves and turn de handle of de grease pot, and when she empty, fill she up again.* Thomas went through the motions of pushing the grease through while his brain was working overtime. When he was done, he left the engine room and came to see me.

"I done what you aks, but Skip, what dat ting for?"

"What thing, the grease pot?"

"Yes, Skip."

"Well, it is there to pump grease into the stuffing box."

"How, Skip?"

"Well, Thomas, as I have explained before, when you open one of the valves in the tubes and turn the handle of the grease pot, the grease flows through the tube and is pushed into the stuffing box."

"I don't tink so, Skip."

"What do you mean, you don't tink so?" Agitated I picked up his accent.

"Well, Skip, dose tubes dey don't go anywhere."

I suddenly got a sick feeling in my stomach. I called Raphael. "Raphael you take the wheel, Thomas and I have a little business in the engine room." I stepped away from the wheel as Raphael took over. "Let's go, Thomas." I pushed our engineer ahead of me toward the stairs leading down into the engine space. The grease pot was located in the aft section of the space, about two feet above the steel floor boards. I studied the contraption and looked down into the opening that was cut into the floor board and through which the copper grease pipes led down under the floors towards the aft end of the ship. To my horror I noticed that both tubes had sheered off where they entered the floor board. A large pile of grease had accumulated directly underneath. Perplexed I looked at Thomas who watched me with an, 'I told you so', smirk on his face.

"See what I mean, Skip. How can de grease get to de stuffing box?"

"Thomas," I snapped, "how long has this been going on?"

"Oh, long time Skip, long time."

"What's a long time?" I questioned desperately, 'Days, weeks, months?"

"Don't know Skip, long time."

Judging by the amount of grease lying in the bilge, I estimated that the tubes had been broken for at least a month - a long, long time!

I had no way of telling how much damage, if any, had been done. To be on the safe side, we stopped the engine and hoisted the sails. What would have been a short trip under power now became a long stretch under sail since the wind was against us, forcing us to tack up Drake's Passage. We zig zagged eastwards up the relatively narrow straight and finally sailed into the harbour at Road Town. The entrance into Village Key Marina was too tight for a boat of *Ring's* size, so we dropped the sails just before we arrived there, and launched our Boston Whaler. With the Whaler snugly tied alongside and the big outboard purring, we managed to slowly manoeuvre *Ring Andersen* safely alongside the dock. I breathed a sigh of relief when after repairing the grease tubes and pumping a large amount of grease into the stuffing box, we discovered during a short sea trial that everything was operating normally. From that day onwards, Thomas diligently checked each time he turned the grease pot to make certain that the grease went into the stuffing box and not into the bilge.

Thomas was in his middle twenties, tall, well proportioned, his perfect set of white teeth highlighted by a handsome, dark skinned face. Thomas's handsome features didn't go unnoticed by the ladies. The saying 'a different girl in every port' most certainly applied to Thomas. Every harbour we sailed into, a girl would be waiting for his arrival. Departures were accompanied with sad farewells from local beauties whose good byes and waving arms could be heard and seen for some time as the shore fell away behind our stern.

Thomas's popularity with the opposite sex became a

problem when we added a female member to our crew. The girl was from the United States and had been working on another charter yacht. She was an attractive, blonde haired young lady who was a capable worker with a pleasant disposition. She was desperate for accommodation and needed a ride to the Virgin Islands from where she would return to her homeland. We could use an extra hand in view of a busy charter schedule, and as companion for Jules, because once our charters were finished, I had to leave the yacht for a period of time to attend to some business in Europe. It didn't take long for our newly hired hand to receive the undivided attention from the male contingent of our crew. Thomas, as I found out later, was making headway with his advances. He was somewhat ahead of Raphael, our boatswain, who also vied for attention. Raphael's nickname was Canejuice as a result of his exploit as a youth in a rum factory where he became thoroughly intoxicated. Canejuice had an artificial leg which he was fitted with after his real leg became badly injured in a motorcycle accident.

Our first set of charters had been carried out successfully. We had a two week reprieve until the next series of charters were to begin. I took the opportunity to go on my business trip and had left the yacht anchored in the bay at West End, Tortola. During my absence the crew would be carrying out routine maintenance and preparing the yacht for the next charters. It was during this period that Jules had to exercise her authority as the Captain's wife.

The daily chores had been performed, the evening meal had been consumed, and the inhabitants of *Ring Andersen* settled in for a quiet night under the tropical stars. Jules was curled up in her bunk with a good book and the crew had retired for the night. Suddenly, Jules heard a commotion on deck. She threw on some clothes and went up to investigate. When she arrived at the location were the disturbance was taking place, she saw Thomas standing at the forward end of the deckhouse, straining to pull something from the roof. Suddenly the object let go, Thomas fell backwards, and the thing he had been pulling on flew up into the air, made an arch, and plunged into the water ten feet away from the yacht's hull. Then the face of Canejuice appeared over the edge of the deckhouse roof. He was watching the projectile that was now floating in the water. When Jules took a closer look in the darkness, she noticed that our female crew member was also on top of the deckhouse. Thomas had picked himself up from the deck and was also looking sheepishly at the thing that was floating in the water. Simultaneously, Canejuice lowered himself from the deckhouse, he only had one leg! Jules now paid closer attention to the dark shape in the water, and sure enough, it was Raphael's artificial limb! Jules turned to Thomas and yelled, "Don't stand there looking at it. Go and get it!"

"Me?' Thomas replied, "Why me?"

"Yes you, you dimwit, you pulled it off. Now you go after it this instant!"

Hesitantly, Thomas started to take off his t-shirt.

"Never mind getting undressed, over the side with you, now, you idiot!" Jules gave him a push in the right direction.

Encouraged by this outburst, Thomas jumped over the side and went in pursuit of the leg. Jules turned to

Raphael and the girl, who had come down from the deckhouse. Raphael stood on his remaining limb, supporting himself against the bullwarks. He looked down sheepishly and embarrassed.

"What in the blazes is going on here?" Jules demanded from the couple.

Apparently, the girl had decided to spend the night on top of the deckhouse where the temperature was cooler than in her cabin. Her location had been noticed by Raphael who was in a romantic mood and thought that she might enjoy some company. However, this had not gone unnoticed by his rival. Thomas had followed him and tried to physically remove him from the object of their affection. A struggle had ensued. Raphael, already on the roof, tried to push Thomas, who was standing on the ladder, away from him with his legs. Thomas held on, grasped a leg and started to pull. Obviously, the strap holding it in place gave away under the strain, resulting in the launch of the projectile.

The limb, now recovered, was returned to its rightful owner and Jules laid down the law.

"You, young lady, you go to your cabin and stay there. No more sleeping on deck, you hear?"

"You, Raphael, you are our boatswain and should know better. And you, Thomas, you do your womanizing on shore and not on this ship!"

The Captain's wife had spoken, and that was the end of that little episode.

Pirates?

When we think of the Caribbean we often think of pirates - Long John Silver, Captain Hook, Black Beard. But the days of pieces of eight, rubies, and other exotic treasure are gone. The pirates feared now are not the legendary types with eye patches, wooden legs and parrots on their shoulders. Today's pirates are those involved in running dope and stealing from cruising yachts. Some cruising folks are so obsessed with pirates that they carry firearms onboard to defend themselves.

Some years ago a cruising yacht arrived in Grenada with armament that ranged from machine guns to flame throwers and hand grenades. As the stuff was taken off the boat for cataloguing and transport to the local police station where it would be kept until the yacht's departure, one of the curious bystanders asked the yacht's occupants what their final destination was. The answer was "New York." We all agreed that in that case they had good reason to arm themselves, but they certainly wouldn't need such weapons in the West Indies.

On the other hand, I heard a tale about an alert Customs officer in St. Lucia who discovered that the occupants of the yacht arriving were not the same as those who had left some days earlier from Trinidad where the boat had been cleared out, bound for St. Lucia. A switch had been made somewhere along the route. Indeed, further investigation revealed that the arriving group were bandits who had disposed of the original occupants at sea.

There are also reports of modern day pirates off the coast of Columbia. In fact, a couple by the name of Bill and Jill Penny in their sailboat *Echo*, were chased by some of those culprits. Six men in an open speedboat chased them when they were making their way to sea, away from the coast. Fortunately, the wind was blowing hard and the water was quite choppy. As they punched to windward with all sails up and the engine going at full throttle, the pursuers had to give up because their boat took on too much water. '

I also remember an incident where a bareboat disappeared from the Windward Islands and was later found sitting in a marina in Fort Lauderdale, Florida. Presumably, the boat had been used for smuggling dope and was abandoned upon completion of the job.

Yes, according to reports, I suppose some form of piracy still does exist, but in reality, in the twentieth century, one would have more of a chance of being hit by a car when walking along the road in a quiet neighbourhood in the USA than to getting attacked by pirates in the Caribbean.

Although firearms are fascinating and interesting mechanisms, as far as I am concerned they are actually somewhat useless. I can't imagine using them to hurt or kill a defenceless animal and in most countries, at least during times of peace, it is against the law to shoot people (and that includes the ones I don't like; even politicians are off limits). So, that leaves the weapon to be cleaned, polished , stroked and looked at and put away again in a safe place, gun and bullets well separated. I've always felt that if a situation would arise where drastic measures are required, a flare gun is a pretty good deterrent while at the same time it doesn't drive the port authorities into a frenzy.

Having said that I must admit that I almost had a gun onboard. I wanted it onboard because I didn't know what else to do with it. I had owned it for many years before coming to the Caribbean. The gun was stored at the home of one of my friends in Vancouver. They said, "Get it out of here, we don't want it." Consequently, during one of my visits to Vancouver I went to the police, obtained a permit to transport it and brought it with me to the airport. When there, I had to check it in with the airline. It could not go with the luggage, it had to be under the care of the pilot who, since I had to change planes a few times, would pass it on to the next pilot, who in turn would pass it on to the next, and so on and so on.

The gun was a Colt 45 with a long barrel, eight inches if I remember correctly. I had bought it at the insistence of a friend who was a bit of a collector. The gun was a classic of the old cowboy movie type. For the purpose of transportation on the plane I had stuffed it into a cardboard box and wrapped that with duct tape.

Ring Andersen was in Tortola, in the British Virgin Islands. My flight from Vancouver was booked with Air Canada, then overnight somewhere in the U.S. Then with Eastern Airlines to San Juan, Puerto Rico, then another flight to St. Thomas, and from there with a local airline to Beef Island Airport in the B.V.I. When I arrived and collected my luggage, the gun was gone. I went to the representative of the airline, then to Customs and reported the missing item. I filled out forms, describing the parcel and the weapon and was told to check back the following day. The next day I went back to the airport, talked to the airline clerk and the Custom's officer. No result. I called Air Canada, then Eastern Airlines, then the airline that had taken me from Puerto Rico to St. Thomas. Each said the parcel with the gun had been passed on to the next flight; therefore, they were not responsible. The following day I went back again to the airport. This time I was advised that the package had been found. It had been miraculously discovered in the area where the baggage normally is deposited upon arrival from the aircraft. "It is somewhere near the conveyor belt. Go look for it." Relieved I went to that section of the building where the luggage arrives from the planes. There it was: I could spot it from a distance lying amongst some other unclaimed items. I picked it up and noticed the tape ripped off, one side of the cardboard box was torn open... The gun was missing! I could feel the Custom's officer's eyes trained on my back. When I turned and looked at him, he quickly avoided my stare and pretended not to have noticed me. I can't prove this of course, and I've probably got it wrong, but at that time I had the strong suspicion that he knew the package was empty. With the empty package in my hand I approached him and said, "It's empty. The gun has been stolen." He gave no reply and he wouldn't look me in the eyes either. He nervously pulled some papers from his shirt's breast pocket, looked at them and then shuffled them back into his pocket. I think he had the gun, but there wasn't anything I could do about it.

The next day we heard on the radio that someone on the island had been shot. It was talked about in the local pubs at great length. Later on in the day we read in the paper that the fellow had been shot with a calibre 45 bullet. The police were looking for the weapon. Jules read the article to me and after she put down the paper she said, "What if it was your gun?" Astonished, I put down the cup of coffee I was just about to put to my lips.

"My gun?"

"Yes, it was a 45 wasn't it? You think the Custom's man took it, but what if he didn't, or what if he sold it or gave it to someone else?"

"That's a bit far fetched isn't it? But then again, who knows, anything is possible."

We both fell silent for a while, each to our own thoughts.

"I don't like this at all." Jules broke the silence. "That thing is registered in your name; everybody who works in the airport knows by now that you brought a gun onto the island. Who knows what crazy ideas they'll come up with? They might say it's your fault, we don't belong here and they might want to blame it on someone who doesn't belong to the local clan."

"You've got a point there," I said. "It could draw us into an investigation that could keep us tied up to the dock for a while."

"I think you should go and see Driscol," Jules said. She was referring to a local lawyer whom we had met via mutual friends.

Half an hour later I was in the law office explaining my predicament.

"There is definitely cause for concern here," the legal beagle said. "We'll draw up a statement which certifies that the last time you had the gun in your possession was in Vancouver two days prior to arrival in Tortola. We'll attach copies of your airline ticket and baggage claims and we'll also advise the authorities in Canada."

"And that will do it?"

"Most certainly, that'll be the end of it."

In retrospect, not having the thing on board probably saved us a lot of hassle with the authorities in the various islands. When I come to think of it, what possessed me to ever acquire it?

Except...

Some weeks later we were cruising in the Windward Islands under a light breeze of about fifteen knots. The sea was calm and *Ring Andersen* was comfortably settled on her course. A straight and foamy wake left behind the stern marked the steady path being carved through the shimmering blue waters of the Caribbean Sea.

As guest on board we had Mr. Fred Zendor, Hollywood film producer, who was scanning the scene for his new production 'The Island' - like Jaws another Peter Benchley story. Incidentally, if you watched this movie (The Island), I would like you to know that the heavy breathing prominent in the under water scenes is by courtesy of Lindy, a charming young lady who for a while served as stewardess on board *Ring Andersen*.

Mr. Zendor, a friendly and interesting gent in his late fifties was accompanied by two well known male movie stars whose names I am not at liberty to mention. Suffice t to say that both gentlemen usually occupied roles of a macho capacity. The two stars were accompanied by two very attractive ladies who were also engaged in the movie industry in some form or another.

As I mentioned, we were cruising at a leisurely pace, the guests were enjoying the sail, the crew was busy with the various tasks onboard and my job at the wheel was easy and uneventful when suddenly I spotted a curious looking vessel.

It was a square rigged sailing vessel, which in itself wasn't all that unusual in these waters; what made her unusual was the dilapidated state of her rigging. The sails were torn and flapping loose in the wind. One of her masts was broken and her hull looked in disrepair. The vessel appeared to be adrift and out of control. Picking up the binoculars I studied her and noticed three men standing on her decks looking into our direction. As we approached they waved frantically; obviously they needed assistance.

I steered *Ring Andersen* toward her, instructing my crew to lower our head sails and mizzen to slow us down. With the main sail still pushing us along at a slow pace I brought *Ring Andersen* within close range of the ill stricken vessel. I noticed that as we came closer more people appeared on the decks of the other vessel. They were a motley looking crew, waving their arms, and yelling at us, crying for help.

Our guests had gathered on deck and stood watching the spectacle. When our hull sides passed within about six feet, suddenly, grapnels and cables shot out from the other ship tying her along side of us. With a deafening tumult of shrill yells and shouts, the men started to climb our bulwarks, wielding swords and cutlasses. They threw themselves upon my crew who desperately struggled to defend themselves. The fighting moved to the foredeck to where my crew had withdrawn. I saw 'Mankind' with a belaying pin in one hand, and a marlin spike in the other, clobber the head of one of the attackers while piercing the chest of another with the spike. Both men fell down, blood was pouring from their wounds, staining the decks. Mankind had a devilish grin on his face as he started on yet another attacker. Near the bowsprit, Raphael had tied himself to a cleat on the railing to support himself while standing on his one good leg, the other, the artificial limb, was in his hands being wielded about like a club. Thomas stood on the focs'l trunk pounding the head of one of the attackers with a winch handle while Twin, in the galley, was fending off an attacker with a wooden dough roller. I didn't see Rock or Vibert and assumed that they were engaged on the other side of the deckhouse from where shouts and sounds of steel clashing against steel could be heard. Hopefully Jules and Michelle had locked themselves below. Suddenly I spotted another wave of men climbing our bullwarks. I quickly jumped down from my position at the wheel and ran to the main sheet winch. I cranked it in, pulling the mainsail hard to windward. Then I released the sheet off the winch and let it fly. I managed to grab the boom and lifted myself, feet sticking out in front of me. With the wind pushing against the sail, the boom flew outward, over the bulwarks, wiping the boarders clean off and into the water. The few remaining scoundrels I kicked off, aided my the momentum of the boom. They fell in between the two vessels, I heard their cries for help.

As I swung past the deckhouse I heard applause and a shout coming from above me. "Well done!" someone yelled. From the corner of my eye I spotted Fred Zendor, the movie producer, standing on the deckhouse roof. He had a camera in his hand and was filming the battle. The two macho stars stood cowering behind him. Incredibly, the pretty ladies were on the deckhouse too, sunning themselves, Aubrey, our steward, was serving them margaritas.

"Help us," I yelled at them.

"Sorry," Mr. Zendor answered, "this is too good an opportunity to miss." He kept on filming.

Then a new group climbed onto the bulwarks and jumped onto our decks. When I saw the guy with the patch over his eye and a parrot on his shoulder I knew that we were done for. Wielding a scabbard in his right hand and a bottle of rum in his left he stood on the railing and yelled, "Arrgh, avast their me hearties." With a nasty grin on his face he threw away the bottle of rum and jumped towards me. *If only I had that gun which was stolen from me on the flight to Tortola*, I thought. I managed to hastily grab a boat hook and lashed out at him. Too late! His scabbard sliced my boat hook in half as I stepped back and tripped over a cleat. I fell backwards onto the deck. As I was fending myself off with the broken boat hook, I caught a glance of Mr. Zendor, still filming, his camera now aimed at me.

"Help us!" I cried out again.

"No can do," Fred Zendor answered. "Too busy!" He carried on filming while I slowly lost consciousness. I kept thinking about that gun, *I should have bought another*

one. It is in circumstances such as this that a yachtie needs a
gun...

The parrot had now flown off the pirate's shoulder
and was perched on my nose, its wings flapping against
my face. I faintly attempted to push the bird's feathers
away, then I heard someone laugh.

When I woke up and looked around me, Jules stood
over me, tickling my face with the edge of a scarf. "Wake
up, " she laughed, "Raphael wants you."

Miffed, I struggled into an upright position and noticed
our guests sitting around a table playing cards. I felt the
smooth surface of the varnish on the seating area of the
aft deck where I had fallen asleep.

"Are you all right?" I said. "Have they gone? Where is
the other ship?"

"Of course we are all right," Jules said. "What other
ship? You must have been dreaming. Raphael is at the
wheel, he needs to see you."

Dazed, I stood up and surveyed the decks. No bodies,
no blood! I walked to the steering station where Raphael
was standing with his artificial leg securely positioned
where it belonged.

"Hello Skip," he said. "Had a good nap?"

Avoiding the question I said, "What's up?"

"See that boat out there Skip?" He pointed ahead a
little to starboard of our course. "She looking strange
Skip, something wrong going on." He handed me the
binoculars.

This was a major deja vu. I could see the vessel was
drifting aimlessly. Three men stood on deck waving
trying to attract our attention. "This can't be," I
mumbled.

"What you say, Skip?"

"Listen closely Canejuice," I said addressing Raphael by his nickname. "They are not going to get us this time. Call the crew. We are going to have a little talk."

Somewhat puzzled, Raphael left and I took the wheel. Again I studied the vessel through the binoculars. This ship was different, smaller and not a sailing ship. I guessed her to be a working boat of about sixty feet in length. She carried a short mast with what appeared to be a cargo boom. There was a deckhouse aft; presumably the wheel house. Cargo hatches where visible further forward. She looked like a local type but not from around the islands further south perhaps. I had never seen her before. As I put the binoculars down the crew gathered around me.

"Listen," I said. "There is a boat ahead of us which apparently needs assistance. I want each one of you to look at her through the binoculars. Study her closely and let me know if you've ever seen her before."

Heads shook as the binoculars were passed from hand to hand.

"Never seen dat boat before, Skip. She not from around here," was the general consensus.

"That's what I thought too." I said.

"Maybe she's from Venezuala?" one of them suggested.

"You could be right," I answered, "but then, what is he doing way up here. Smuggling perhaps? On her way to, or back from a trip to St. Barts? Or, Petit Martinique perhaps?" Both islands were known to be frequented by smugglers. Mostly for cheap booze and cigarettes. "I don't trust them. Let's handle this very carefully. Take both jibs and staysail down and also the mizzen. That will slow us down, then we will go in for a closer look."

Something flashed in my mind, this action sounded vaguely familiar.

"On second thought," I called after the departing crew "take the mainsail down too, and Thomas, start the engine!"

The sails came down and *Ring Andersen* began to check her speed. The familiar huffing, hissing and puffing could be heard as Thomas, alias Steambox, put the air through the system and the big flywheel of our Volund started to turn. Shee-ka-boo, shee-ka-boo, I turned the propeller to low pitch forward and engaged the clutch. Our passengers were gathered on deck watching the proceedings.

We were now coming closer. When we were within fifty feet I started to circle the vessel, well out of range of grapnels.

"What's the problem?" I yelled at the men who were still standing on her decks.

"Our engine is broken down and we are making water," came the reply. I could detect a Spanish accent.

"We'll throw you a line and tow you to Carriacou!" Tyrell Bay in Carriacou was the closest harbour.

"No Capitan, we want to come on board with you we are afraid she's going to sink!"

"How many of you are there?"

"Just us," one of the men said.

Just us, I thought, *that can mean the three on deck, or more, hidden below*. I turned to Jules who was standing beside me.

"Get the flare pistol from the chart room.. Make sure there's a cartridge in it." Then, noticing Thomas standing at the entrance to the engine room I said, "Thomas ge that steel bar that you use to crank the flywheel."

Jules returned with the pistol and Thomas ascended from the engine room with the steel bar.

The rest of the crew had come back from their chores of securing the sails and now stood near me. I explained my plan:

"Okay, this is how we'll do this. We will stand off to windward no closer than thirty feet from them. As soon as we're in position, launch one of the boats and let it drift out to them so they can board it. Then we'll pull them in and let them board *Ring* one by one. As they arrive I want them to lie down and you guys search for weapons. Thomas will stand nearby with his steel bar and I will stand ready with the flare pistol. Jules will stay at the wheel and keep us in position. Be careful - I don't trust these guys."

"Skip," Mankind commented, "I tink day is lying, dat boat not making much water, look at de waterline, it look okay."

He was right. If the ship had taken on a lot of water, the waterline would have been low or not visible, but there was no sign of any buoyancy irregularities.

I said, "Okay, let's take our posts."

I manoeuvred *Ring* to windward of the other vessel and gave the sign to lower the shore boat. Raphael paid out the line until the boat drifted against the hull of the small freighter. Immediately the three men I had seen on her decks started to board. Just as number three stepped in I saw four others come out of the wheel house, rushing for our shore boat. Before I could say anything Raphael had already taken action. He heaved on the line and the small boat pulled away from the cargo vessel, the third man just barely able to get in and almost losing his balance.

"Good show, Raphael!" I shouted and ran towards the gate while Jules took my place at the wheel. The other four, now joined by two more, stood sheepishly looking at our shore boat as it was pulled alongside *Ring*. Vibert and Rock physically pulled one of the occupants from the boat onto *Ring's* deck. Pointing the flare gun at him I said, "Get down onto the deck, face down!" Staring at my gun with fright the fellow did as I commanded. The other two were still in the shore boat, Thomas standing above them at the gate, his steel bar raised and ready. Vibert and Rock had started to frisk our prisoner pulling a large machete from his baggy trousers. The thing had been well hidden along the side of his right leg.

"Okay, I've seen enough," I said. "Get back into the boat and we'll put you back onboard your own ship. If your boat is leaking, she won't sink before we have towed you to Tyrell Bay. There you can beach her on the sand."

The fellow seemed eager to get back with his pals, for he immediately stood up and jumped into the shore boat.

"Let the boat drift back, Raphael," I said. "Don't give them a chance to tie it up along side theirs, we don't want them to take it."

"No problem Skip, I'll pull back as soon as they do something I don't like."

All our eyes were trained on the boat as it slowly drifted to the other vessel.

I now pointed the flare gun at the men onboard and yelled, "Don't try anything funny, I'll shoot if I have to and set your ship on fire. As soon as your men are onboard we'll throw you a line and tow you to Tyrell

Bay. That is, if you still think you need assistance."

There was no reply. Our boat came in contact with the cargo boat and the men jumped out, onto their own vessel. The very second the last one grabbed onto her railing, Raphael pulled our shore boat away from under his feet. For a moment I thought the fellow would fall into the water but he was grabbed by his mates just in time.

Our boat was retrieved and hauled up in the davits. As it came out of the water, we suddenly heard the engine of the 'stricken' vessel start up with a roar and then take off at great speed.

Fred Zendor broke the silence as we watched them disappear in an westerly direction, away from land. "Wow," he said "That was a close call." I couldn't have agreed with him more.

I called the authorities in both St.Vincent and Grenada and gave them a description of the vessel. I also tuned to 2638, the charter yacht channel, and advised all yachts about our encounter. After that we made sail and continued on our way.

I guess I didn't need that gun after all. A flare pistol will do the trick and it's legal to carry onboard.

Greener Grass

Reading the tales recorded in this book may lead the reader into believing that operating a charter yacht in the West Indies is all sunshine and roses. Don't be deceived! No, we are not all running around with a glass of rum punch in the hand and a hibiscus behind the ear. In addition to hard work in maintaining the boat, the shopping for, and the subsequent coming onboard of dinghy loads full of provisions which require stowing in relatively little space, there are the typical West Indian idiosyncrasies that have to be dealt with. On the subject of shopping, for instance, when arriving at the store it is not uncommon to find the door locked with the display of a sign that states 'Gone to come back'. This means that the shopkeeper may have stepped out for a minute and will return shortly, or has left the country and 'won't be back for many a day'.

We are not dealing here with North American supermarkets. Although the stores may be large and modern looking, the staff and management are West Indian. Whereas in America, items that are sold are faithfully recorded and subtracted from the inventory, thus allowing the ordering of new supplies well in advance and before they run out, such is not the case in the West Indies. As a rule, stock is sold until it runs out. Then, maybe new goods are ordered. At the present, with the aid of computers, that may no longer be so, but it certainly was the case in the seventies.

Much of the merchandise has to be imported from other countries. Since the remoteness of the islands cause considerable delay in shipping, it was therefore not unusual that an island would run out of a certain product for long periods of time. At one time in Nassau, in the Bahamas, the entire island had run out of sugar. Even the surrounding islands had none available. A commodity like this is important for a charter yacht and the unavailability of it causes the operators much frustration. Certain goods which we take for granted in North America are not, or certainly during the seventies were not, available. Real milk, fresh eggs, and western fruits such as apples, pears, strawberries and so on could not be bought on most of the islands. Apples were sometimes imported, but they were expensive and by the time they arrived in the islands, hardly edible. I sometimes got cravings for a nice juicy apple.

At one time, while alongside the dock in Grenada, I spotted an apple floating in the water. My daughter Michele had seen it too. We both poked with boat hooks, and eventually with a fishing net, we retrieved it from the water. When we had it onboard, we examined it carefully with our mouths watering. It was a big, juicy looking apple and we reasoned that it must have fallen off a cruise ship. We washed it and polished it and then put it in a prominent spot on the varnished coaming of the steering station for further study. I had to promise

Michele not to touch it while she went to the galley to fetch a knife. She came back with a knife, two saucers, two napkins and a table cloth. The cloth was spread on the table which lived on the aft deck. Carefully, the apple was transported to the center of the table cloth. The two saucers were put at the opposite ends of the table. We sat down and started to carefully plan were the incision should be made. After much deliberation a spot was chosen where upon Michele expertly sliced the apple in half. I was licking my lips in anticipation as Michele performed the operation. We closed our eyes when, finally, we took the first bite of this heavenly delicacy, groaning with pleasure as the fruit's flesh tickled our taste buds.

No other apple I have eaten since tasted as good as that one.

The milk available in the islands was a product called 'Stay Fresh'. I don't know how it was made, but whatever chemicals were in it, they prevented the liquid from going off even after the cardboard container had been opened and left standing in the tropical heat for days. It somewhat resembled the taste of milk, was acceptable in coffee and could be used for baking and cooking purposes, but it was absolutely useless for the production of good ice cream. At that time, most of the ice cream available tasted watery with distinct flavour overtones of sugar cane. The American Virgin Islands didn't have this problem. They were regularly supplied from the U.S.A. Since I have a weakness for ice cream, every time we arrived in St. Thomas, even before reporting to the Customs office, I would con Jules in sneaking off for a detour which lead us to Sebastians where they sold delicious strawberry sundaes. After a while, the waitress recognized us when we sat down at a table waiting to be served. "Ha, there you are again! Let me see, that will be a strawberry sundae for the gentleman and a beer for the lady." Giggling, she would depart to fulfill the order.

People living in North America take it for granted that virtually everything they fancy is available at any time, anywhere in their immediate vicinity. When living in the West Indies, one is reminded of this during the occasional visit to a 'sophisticated' city of a more affluent country.

At one time, Haze Richardson of the PSV resort and his then wife Jennifer, and Jules and I organized a trip to Caracas, Venezuela. Haze is an avid flyer and owns an airplane. With Haze at the controls, Jennifer sitting beside him and Jules and I in the back seat, we flew from Union Island to Trinidad, where we stopped for fueling and obtained the necessary papers for entry into Venezuela. The next day we carried on to Caracas. When there, we were overawed by the goods in the stores, the food in the restaurants, and especially the fruit on the market stands. Apples, pears and above all, grapes, real grapes, as large as plums. We walked through the streets with stores displaying merchandise in the brightly lit and well displayed windows, pointing at items we hardly remembered existed. Haze and Jennifer went in one direction and Jules and I in another, agreeing to meet at a certain place at a certain time. Off we went on a shopping frenzy. Suddenly Jules and I walked by a store with men's clothing. In the window I spotted a suit that caught my attention. "Let's take a look inside," I said to

Jules. As soon as we entered though the door a salesman appeared out of nowhere. This in itself was a novelty we weren't accustomed to.

In the West Indies, when one enters a store to look for an item, one of the problems is to find a clerk who is sufficiently motivated to offer service. This often involves scanning the place for any human bodies. Chances are that the one most inactive is an employee of the store. One then approaches this body carefully, making sure to not disturb that person too abruptly. The first question to pose is something like, "Hello, do you work here?" In all probability this will cause the head on the body to slowly open its eyes, study your personage for a while, and then look around to see if the pending job can be passed onto one of the other employees. If no one else is in the vicinity, he or she will shift weight from one leg to the other, some head scratching will occur, followed by a suspicious and hesitant, "Yes?" This should be acted upon with the question, "I am looking for a such and such. Do you have it?" A long pensive look will follow, the eyes thrown skyward in despair, then a nod, or possibly, "I tink so." Having made considerable headway so far, the next question is, "Where can I find it?" More head scratching and eyes casting to the heavens are likely to be a response, after which an arm is raised with the hand pointing vaguely in the vicinity of where the item may be located. "Dat way." The chore thus having been carried out, the employee will get back into his previous position: the weight now shifted to the other leg and somewhat stretched out in front, the back leaning against the wall or display stand, the elbows raised and positioned on a ledge to provide additional support. The chin sinks down to the chest, the eye lids closing slowly.

The owner of the Red Crab, a restaurant and pub in Grenada popular with the yachties, had a sign posted on the wall to assist new comers to the West Indies. It read something like this:

"To distinguish between dead and living employees, those bodies found in a near vertical position are the ones most likely to be alive."

Needless to say, Jules and I were surprised with the prompt appearance of the salesman in the store in Caracas. Immediately noticing that we were strangers he asked in fluent English, "Good afternoon, Signor and Signora, is there anything I can do for you?"

"Well," I said hesitantly, "I was just looking at that suit that is displayed in the window."

"Which one, Signor?" With a flourish he withdrew the door of the display case.

"That one," pointing to the suit I had seen from the street.

"Ha, that one, just one moment." He jumped onto the display counter and removed the suit from the dummy. Before I knew it, he had slipped the jacket over my arms and shoulders. He stepped back and looked me over, commenting that the jacket hung nicely around me. Promptly, another clerk appeared with a tall mirror on rollers. As the first clerk fussed to straighten the collar, while removing some imaginary dust from the shoulders and giving a tug here and there, the other gent positioned the mirror in front of me. I was admiring myself in the mirror, when yet another man appeared. With chalk he made some marks on the back of the jacket and then I was hustled into a dressing room to try on the pants.

When I came out, the trio was waiting, more chalk marks were made and in the mean time, one of the clerks had moved over to Jules with a selection of socks, neckties and shirts. Jules by this time had been positioned in a chair and was looking on as the fellow moved back and forth from her to me, each time holding up a shirt and a tie, alternately displaying the items under my chin. I hadn't been able to utter a word when the pronouncement came that the suit would be altered and ready for pickup in two hours time, together with a pair of socks, a shirt, and a matching tie. Perplexed, I paid the bill that was handed to me.

I still have that suit; there have been no occasions for me to wear it. In fact, I rarely wear suits, I dislike wearing suits, but that suit is a nice suit and one of these days I might put it on, if it still fits. Come to think of it, the trousers have bell bottoms!

Gone to Come Back

Sooner or later, all good things come to an end. The charter business was changing. I could see that the future of the luxury, crewed charter yacht, especially those built of wood, would soon be a thing of the past. Wooden yachts with their high cost of maintenance were destined to have a hard time surviving in a forever changing world. It was time to say good bye to the old girl and put *Ring Andersen* up for sale.

Within weeks, a prospective buyer chartered us to get a feel for the yacht.

While *Ring* is by no means a racing yacht, and slow to tack and a handful to maneuver in close quarters, she can move when the conditions are right. We once set records during a trip from St. Vincent to Petit St. Vincent, and again the next day under similar conditions from P.S.V. to Grenada. We averaged just over fourteen and a half knots, and for short intervals I observed her speed exceeding sixteen knots. These were exciting trips, with the crew cheering, the rigging taut and vibrating - humming out its own song, the water churned to white foam, leaving a long straight wake behind us.

With the prospective buyer onboard during one

portion of the trip, the wind built up to a good thirty knots and *Ring* was showing her stuff, he was elated by her performance. As we stood at the bow, *Ring* charging ahead like a locomotive, white foam flying along her hull sides, he made up his mind and decided he had to have her. Thus my pride and joy was sold to an owner who had the resources to keep her in top notch condition without having to rely on charter income. Shortly after the verbal agreement was made I left for New York to meet with the new owner's lawyers and complete the transaction. This firm of lawyers discovered that, unbeknownst to me, there was a lien against *Ring* in Panama. Apparently, before I bought her, the yacht had at one time been leased to a gentleman who had started to register her under the Panamanian Flag. How this had been possible without him having ownership remains a mystery. The registration had apparently been abandoned somewhere along the process, but in the mean time, certain expenses had been accumulated which had been accrued against the boat. I suppose I was lucky that sometime ago, when I planned a voyage to Vancouver, plans had changed and the trip was never undertaken. If it had, I certainly would have been in big trouble when negotiating the Panama Canal.

At first, after the sale had been completed, we remained on board to operate her on the owner's behalf. But that turned out not to be a good idea. There were too many memories, there was too much pride of ownership. I was too possessive of my cherished *Ring Andersen*. In her we had put so much sweat, so much labour of love, and with her we had covered so much distance over such a long time. I realized my predicament when at one time I got

Like a locomotive

On deck, J.P. at the wheel

Sunset at sea

angry with the new owner for damaging one of my favourite chairs. "But, this is my chair," he said. "I now own this boat."

Jules and I stayed on board until a new skipper was settled in and then went on to other things.

It is often said that the two happiest days in a boat owners life are the day the boat is bought and the day she is sold. That may apply to some but definitely not to me. Saying good bye to *Ring* was like closing a door on part of my life, like losing a close member of the family. It hurt!

It was tough on the crew, too. We had been together for many years. They were convinced I would soon re-appear on the scene with another boat. I had made an arrangement with the new owner and his skipper that the crew would remain employed on the yacht, but I had a heck of a time convincing the guys that they should stay onboard. "Are you sure you won't have another yacht, Skip?" Unconvinced they signed on with the new skipper. Two months later they were back in Grenada, expecting I would have another boat waiting for them.

I'm sad to say that along with *Ring Andersen*, the majority of the great yachts have disappeared from the West Indian charter scene. Gone are boats like *Orphee, Lord Jim, Ticonderoga, Ariels, Mizar, Snark, Puritan, Grace, Cariad, Zorra*, and others. Some are still sailing and in good condition, others are in disrepair or lying at the bottom of the ocean. This large fleet of magnificent and majestic sailing yachts is now replaced by plastic bareboats.

Jules and I bought a 57 ft. sloop, and yes, we stooped to the reasons of logic and economics, for she was built of fibreglass. The boat was easy to maintain and sailing her was quite manageable for the two of us. She was a Columbia 57. We named her *Lioness*. She proved to be very seaworthy and fast. We bid our farewells to the West Indies and started cruising.

Our trip went smoothly and without any harrowing experiences. Eventually, some two years later, heading for Vancouver, we cruised up along the West Coast of the North American continent. We stayed close to the coast and frequently stopped at ports along the way for sight seeing. This is what cruising is all about: harbour hopping, from port to port, enjoying new places and meeting the locals.

An interesting phenomenon about the trip along the West Coast is that there seems to be a school of thought that suggests that it is better to stay some two hundred and fifty miles off shore. This having to do something with prevailing winds and sea conditions. This theory has never made any sense to me. The sea condition is notoriously worse further out as can be verified by the weather reports broadcasted continuously on the VHF. Furthermore, if it gets too rough, once caught two hundred and fifty miles out, it is a long run in to find shelter. Also, most ports along the coast close down in heavy weather when the harbour entrances are too dangerous for navigation. Yet, if one stays close to the coast one can get inside before the wind and seas turn into turmoil. I also don't understand why anyone would want to add five hundred miles, two hundred and fifty out and two hundred and fifty back, to a voyage on a stretch of ocean which can be quite hostile and bitterly cold! I remembered having negotiated this coast on freighters and standing on the bridge watching the traffic on the coastal highway not too many miles away. Why take a different route on a small boat?

We played the weather by checking the forecast and only continued when there was a 'window' of favourable winds and reasonably calm seas. Only then would we continue, bound for the next port. Even this can be deceiving.

We had spent some time in Eureka, California, a splendid city with many historical buildings and where we had been royally welcomed by some of the local yachties. When the time came to continue our journey the barometer was steady, the sky blue, and the wind about fifteen knots. Ideal sailing weather. We cast off our lines and headed towards the channel that would take us out into the Pacific Ocean. Just before coming to the entrance my attention was distracted by a large vessel which was anchored at the mouth of the channel. It was rolling and spewing mud. Barges were lying alongside. It was obviously dredging that part of the harbour. I was fascinated by the vessel's motion and the workings of the buckets as they retrieved the mud from the bottom. Thus distracted I failed to notice the huge rollers coming in through the channel entrance. I also failed to observe the posted signal which indicated that the entrance was unsafe for navigation and closed. I didn't spot the condition until it was too late and we were in it. Too late to turn back and risk the danger of being broad-sided by one of those rollers. We had to press on! Our situation was confirmed when Jules, who had wedged herself halfway down the companionway, her eyes just above the sliding hatch, heard a message on the VHF radio.

Someone on the dredger was calling the Coast Guard, telling them to stand by. There was a yacht in the channel!

"They are talking about us," Jules shouted, barely audible above the noise of *Lioness* crashing into the heavy seas.

"Hang on," I yelled, "we are committed now, we can't turn back. It will ease off once we get outside in deeper water." I played the throttle, speeding up as we climbed another roller, slowing down as we descended and then climbing the next wave at a slight angle until turning into it, head on, as we neared the top. At times I thought the engine would not be able to give us the power to push the boat up against the steep angle of the seas. I automatically leaned and pressed against the steering pedestal as if that would help to push the boat forward. While all this was going on I recalled a photograph hanging in the office of David Fraser, the owner of Fraser Yachts. It portrayed a yacht negotiating this same channel under similar conditions. The deckhouse was sheered off by a crashing wave and subsequently the yacht flipped over backwards and was totally destroyed. I was determined not to come to the same fate.

I continued to meet each wall of water, manipulating the wheel and the throttle. Finally, after what seemed like ages, we left the channel behind us and found ourselves in the ocean. Once outside, we noticed several large fishing vessels hove to, waiting for the seas to subside before entering the port. Even in open water the seas were nasty, short and steep. We later heard that the conditions were caused by a typhoon which had ravaged through the southern Pacific some days before.

Especially during this episode, the boat proved to be

Lioness

first class in design and construction. A lesser vessel might not have survived this nasty experience.

After having visited some more places along the way, we ended up in Vancouver, Canada, and cruised the beautiful islands of the Pacific Northwest. The next year we spent a whole summer in the Queen Charlottes, a mystical and spell binding, isolated group of islands lying off the northwest coast of British Columbia. Due to an abundance of rare species of wildlife, these islands are sometimes referred to as the Galapagos of the North Pacific. There we met Dick, a Haida custodian of the historic village of Ninstints on Anthony island. The place has long been deserted and a visit is somewhat of a religious experience. Rows of ancient totem poles still stand eerily among the tall cedar trees, guarding the remains of the once populated long houses. The spirits of inhabitants from a not so ancient past seem to quietly go about their business amongst the quiet woods, their bodies encased on top of the burial poles. Dick, the custodian, the only living soul there to make certain that visitors didn't disturb artifacts, became our mentor and taught us much about the Haida ways. He knew much about local plants and showed us how a certain type of sea grass, called *Salicornica Pacifica*, can be prepared as a delicious and nourishing vegetable. We were soon living off the land and seabed. As a matter of fact, that was the first trip we had ever taken where our freezer was fuller when we left than when we arrived.

During a moment of confidence, Dick took us to a sacred place where there was evidence of a civilization that according to him, predated the Haida, to a well hidden cave where people had lived and died. In here we saw evidence of food having been prepared and where people had been buried. Remains in the form of bones and skulls were collected in one area. The discovery of this brings forward an interesting speculation. If these remains indeed belonged to a people pre-Haida, it would indicate that the North American Indians were not the first and original inhabitants of this continent as is commonly stated. I can see this bringing forth all kinds of political ramifications that might influence the settlement of aboriginal land claims. The Haida believe they were the first people on earth. Originally, they were locked up in a clam shell. The Raven pried open the shell and liberated them, thus allowing them to freely wander over the earth.

We had ended up in the Queen Charlotte Islands because originally we were contracted to take some of the clientele of a couple that operated a charter business in the area. Their business was a bit different from what we were used to in that instead of providing luxury style cruises, they catered to people who were interested in learning about the ways and customs of the Haida and the environment. The Sierra Club was one of their customers. Al and Irene Whitney operated a company named Pacific Synergies. Their boat, the *Darwin Sound*, was heavily booked and unable to cope with the fast growth of their successful operation. Each cruise was accompanied by a resource person, someone knowledgeable about the area and its people. The most memorable of these was the famous artist, carver and sculptor Bill Reid, who we were lucky enough to have on board during one of the cruises. Bill Reid's artwork can be seen in the Vancouver Airport where a variety of his works are displayed. Also in Vancouver, on the campus of the University of British Columbia, is one of Mr. Reid's most prominent works: a sculpture of the human species struggling to get out of the clamshell as same is being opened by the Raven.

Fascinated by the place we stayed until well after the cruises were finished. Late in the autumn we said goodbye to Dick and his enchanted islands and sailed back to Vancouver.

To be more or less semi-permanently tied up to a dock in a large marina in Vancouver was a bit of a culture shock. We felt out of place and didn't appreciate the hustle and bustle of the big city. We also didn't know where to go from here. A wake-up call came when a person, whom I knew as a friend from many years ago, swindled me out off a large amount of cash. Suddenly, some form of employment became of the utmost importance. I became a marine surveyor again, something I had done in a previous life. If you think being a marine surveyor is a soft and easy job, you are mistaken. Sometimes it can be as scary as hell as I found out on that particular day.

The day was off to a normal start. Two surveys to do. One in the morning and one in the afternoon. I looked at the sheet with particulars prepared by our secretary. First a 36 footer, a power boat, then a 38 foot sailboat in the afternoon. The power boat was to be inspected in a marina in North Vancouver, the sailboat in downtown Vancouver. There was a hand written scribble under the particulars of the sailboat. *'On the way back, would you swing by a private home to take a look at a small power boat located on a trailer'*. Added to this were the comments; 'For evaluation only. A legal case!' The notation ended with the address. *Hm, probably a divorce*, I thought, and put the note away in my pocket.

I enjoy doing marine surveys. It's a nice, quiet and interesting occupation. Dictating the reports is a bit of a bore, but I like doing the actual inspection work. One arrives at the site, goes through the boat, and makes notes about the condition of the vessel. This exercise is often accompanied by the watchful eyes of interested bystanders, be they owners, prospective buyers, or just plain folks who are curious about this fellow who is bashing that nice looking finish of the hull with a hammer. A comment here and there, some friendly chit chat, and then the parting with a warm handshake. Normally that's how it goes, except that Monday!

I finished the second boat at about six P.M. I put my bag of tools in my truck, said good bye to the couple who were contemplating buying the sailboat, and William and I drove away. William, or Willy, as I usually call him, threw me a questioning glance. "No," I said, "we can't go home yet, first we have to do that evaluation." He looked at me with sad eyes. "Yes, I know," I said, "it's dinner time. But this won't take long. It's only a little boat and it's not a full survey." William sighed and curled up on the passenger seat.

As you may have guessed, William is my dog and faithful companion, an addition to the now more or less landlocked family. He is a big dog, a cross between a black lab and a Chesapeake. He weighs in at ninety five pounds and is extremely protective of me. He has also appointed himself as the defender of my truck, my tool bag, and any other paraphernalia that he figures belongs

to me or him. This sometimes includes the boat I am
inspecting. Once I am on board, he won't let anyone
else in, including the rightful owner, unless I explain to
him that that person won't attack me and has a legal
right to be there.

It was almost seven o'clock when we arrived at the
address where the boat was located. I spotted it on the
right hand side of the road, on a trailer, parked in the
driveway of the house. The house was of the style where
the garage is attached to the front; a double garage with a
large overhead door. The door was open and through
the garage I could see a door leading to the inside of the
dwelling. A few other vehicles stood parked beside the
boat on the driveway. One of them was a mini van. I
pulled up onto the driveway and parked in front of the
boat. As I drove in, I noticed a young woman and a man
on the adjacent lot. With them was a tall teenage lad.
They walked toward me as I was getting out of the truck.
William was about to follow me out, but I told him to
wait in the truck. I left the window open a bit for fresh
air.

"Hello," I said to the young woman, "is this the boat
that needs an evaluation?"

"Yes," she answered, "thank you for coming on such
short notice. This is my husband." She pointed to the
gent beside her. She made no reference to the teenager.

We shook hands. I took a note pad and walked to the
stern of the boat to record the serial number. The stern
was nearest to the garage.

"What's he doing?" the teenager asked the husband.

"This man is a marine surveyor. He is going to appraise
the boat. It won't take long."

I sensed animosity between the two, yet the husband and wife seemed quite friendly to one another. *Maybe a friendly divorce,* I thought, and started to remove the canvass cover from the boat. Just then a lady, who I guessed to be in her late forties, came out of the garage.

"What's going on?" she yelled. "What are you doing here?"

I looked at the couple. But they didn't volunteer any information, so I replied, "I have been asked to do an appraisal of this vessel."

"An appraisal? I don't know anything about that. If you are doing an appraisal, you're doing it for me, because this is my boat."

The young woman whispered in my ear, "Don't pay any attention to her, just go ahead and do whatever you have to do."

The other woman overheard this and now yelled at all of us, "Get off my property. This is private property, get off!"

I looked at the young woman and her husband and said, "What's going on here? Is this your boat or isn't it? And isn't this your house?"

"This is our boat and this is our house," the young woman and her husband both replied.

"No it's not," the tall lad now interjected. "You are both effing liars!"

Suddenly, the door in the back of the garage opened and a gray haired man stormed out. "Get the hell off my property!" he yelled. "I have called the police! And," he added to me, "this is my house and this is my boat. I can prove it! I have the registration papers in the house."

Not knowing what to do, I looked from the older to

the younger couple. The young woman said again, "Just go ahead. It's just a bit of a family squabble. Pay no attention."

Probably any sane surveyor at this time would have said, "Goodbye, it was nice meeting you. Call me when you get this sorted out." But, you see, there has always been that nagging yearning deep inside me about wanting to know what lies beyond the next horizon. And an inner voice told me *there is more to come, this isn't your ordinary survey.* Then again, maybe I'm just plain nosy. In any event, against my better judgement, I said to the man with the gray hair,

"Did you say that you called the police?"

"Yes!" he said, challenging.

"Are they on their way, right now?"

"Yes!"

"Good," I said, "then, if you don't mind, I will just wait until they get here and let them sort it out."

This seemed agreeable; at least the man shrugged his shoulders and went back into the house. The woman, his wife, she stayed.

"This is my daughter, you know," she hissed at me, pointing at my would-be client. "Can you imagine that? My own daughter." The young woman rolled her eyes towards the sky and threw her a defiant look in reply.

I lit up a cigarette and moved away from the crowd toward the bow of the boat. I stood there, contemplating the scene, when the younger couple joined me and filled me in on some of the details. Apparently, the daughter and son-in-law had built the house together with the parents. The boat was also jointly purchased. The younger couple had three small children and had been living with the parents in the same house. The teenager was a son of the older couple and the brother of the young woman. According to the young couple, this teenage son had a drug problem. The parents wouldn't do anything about it and the young couple moved out, not wanting to expose their children to the drug scene. Things went downhill from there and got nasty. The house and the boat were to be sold and the proceeds divided. The parents were not cooperating.

I walked back to where the older woman was standing.

"There are two sides to every story, you know," she said to me, aware that her daughter and son-in-law had been chatting with me.

"I realize that," I said, "but it's really none of my business."

I stood between the garage and the boat. Suddenly, a car and a truck drove up. With squealing brakes they halted across the street of the residence. Two sturdy young men in their late twenties stormed out; one of them was swinging a baseball bat.

"Get off this property!" they both yelled.

I wasn't certain to whom they were directing their order. I gathered it was meant for all of us, but the fellow with the baseball bat came running toward me.

"Get the hell off this property!" he yelled again. He swung the bat, getting ready for action.

"Now wait a minute," I exclaimed, taking a step forward and holding up my arm to fend off a blow, "this is going a bit far. Don't you threaten me with that baseball bat. The police are on their way, just simmer down!"

The fellow hesitated, then turned away from me and started to attack the son-in-law.

William, who thus far had been following the whole procedure with keen interest, now went berserk. He knew I was being threatened. His heavy bark exploded from the truck. His prancing around made it shake. He threw himself against the windshield and clawed at the doors. The baseball man and the son-in-law were rolling on the driveway, the teenager was fighting with the other man, the one who had come out of the car. Then the gray haired man bolted out of the garage. "This is all your fault!" he screamed at me. Then he joined in with the fighting. I stepped aside as two bodies, punching and twisting, stumbled toward me. Promptly, I had to step aside again to avoid three fighting bodies, all mangled together. They fell against my truck. I heard a snarl and the tearing of clothes, when William, his jaws through the partially lowered window, managed to get hold of a shoulder passing by the opening. Other bodies, entwined, rolled against the mini van, setting off the burglar alarm. The thing went off with a whine, adding to the noise and tumult that went on around me.

I stood there, still occasionally puffing away on my cigarette, feeling kind of detached, wondering if I should be joining in. Then the police cars arrived, the noise of their sirens in discord with the van's burglar alarm, the thumping, the screaming and the shouting, and William's frantic barking.

Four stout policemen broke up the fight. They divided the opposing parties and started questioning the participants. I gathered from the interrogation that the two men who had arrived in the car and the truck were two other brothers, sons of the gray haired man and his wife. A police woman, who directed part of the interrogation, asked me if I was a relative.

"No," I said, "I am just a marine surveyor. I came to look at that boat." I gave her my card. "If you don't need me just now, I'd like to go home. Perhaps you'd like to call me if necessary." She took my card and agreed to phone me later. I wished her good luck and got into my truck. She gave me a friendly nod and touched her cap politely as she watched me drive away.

William looked at me with his big, faithful, questioning eyes.

"Yes," I said, "we're going home. It's dinner time."

Relieved, he sat down in the passenger seat. Peering through the windshield he watched our progress with keen anticipation.

Jules kept talking about horses, something she had been involved with in her childhood. During one of my surveys I was introduced to Bowen Island, a place I had been to before but never given much thought. This time I was intrigued. Bowen Island lies in the waters of Howe Sound, a fifteen minute ferry ride from Horseshoe Bay and from there a short drive into Vancouver. The island reminded me of the Caribbean, a small, friendly community composed of people from all walks of life with a similar attitude: 'if we can't do it today, we'll do it tomorrow.., maybe'. There was a village type nucleus, called the Cove, where you were bound to run into someone with whom you could strike up an interesting conversation. I mentioned my observations to Hamish Miller, the fellow I was doing a survey for. He immediately made a phone call and a few minutes later I was introduced to Peter Dives, local real estate agent.

The next day I was back on Bowen Island, this time accompanied by Jules. Peter met us at the ferry dock and drove us around, showing the various properties for sale. We ended up falling in love with a small cottage that was situated on a three and a half acre parcel bordering a park and overlooking a lake. I liked the view and closeness of the lake, while Jules visualized her horse grazing on the large expanse of sloping lawn. The price was right and the deal was made.

In the meantime, along with my surveying business, I had started a yacht management company. It started with a seventy-three foot motor yacht that was owned by a businessman from Spokane, U.S.A. Yacht management meant that I supervised the maintenance, had the boat provisioned and ready to go when the owner wanted to go on a cruise, and supplied the necessary manpower, skipper, cook, deckhand, stewardess, etc. The word spread to other owners of big yachts and before long I had a dozen or so large yachts to look after. The majority of these were owned by Americans and the boats were of U.S. registry. This was during the early 1980's and the economy in British Columbia was not too hot, resulting in high unemployment. However, my newly instigated enterprise was flourishing and soon I was employing quite a few yachties who otherwise would have been without income.

The operation attracted the attention of a person by the name of Peter Mandrell who was a government employee with great foresight. Peter was with the department of Development and Tourism and he felt that my operation was of great benefit to the local economy. Not only did it provide employment to the crews operating the boats, but the amount of money spent at local ship yards was phenomenal. Big boats cost a lot of money to maintain! Furthermore, the money that was spent was spent by Americans, thus, U.S. dollars entered the country. When the owners were not using them, the yachts also chartered and brought tourists into the country. Peter recognized the potential and offered his government's full cooperation. We organized a charter yacht show the cost of which was shared equally by me and the government. We were off to a great start until some other dignitaries in the government decided that the operation did not comply with the laws of the land, as became evident during the following incident.

The skipper of one of the boats was onboard getting her ready to take her to the Nanaimo Shipyard. The yacht's owner had told me that he wanted the boat in Mexico for the winter season. Since the boat, a 78 foot sailing yacht, was built of steel and needed to have her bottom painted, I decided that we should haul the boat for a thorough going over before embarking on the long voyage. I contracted with the shipyard to have the boat's bottom sandblasted and coated with epoxy before applying the antifouling paint. The owner had agreed to the cost which was somewhere around thirty thousand dollars.

When the skipper was making some last minute preparations while the yacht was lying alongside the dock in a marina in Vancouver, he was approached by two customs officers. The twosome, young and new with the department, had been looking at the yachts tied up in the marina when they spotted my man on the yacht. Being curious and attracted by this very nice looking vessel, they started a conversation with the skipper. They had noticed the American flag flying on the flag staff and probably assumed that the people on board were from the U.S.

"Where are you form?" one of the rookies said to the busy skipper who was on deck going through a box with fuel filters.

"Me? I live in Vancouver," came the answer.

"You live in Vancouver? Are you not an American citizen?"

"No, I'm Canadian," the skipper answered.

The two officials turned away and held a hurried conference. Then they turned back to our skipper and said, "Are you employed on this boat or are you a guest?"

"Of course I'm employed on this boat. This is my job, I am the skipper. And if you'll excuse me I have to go, I'm running a bit late, we have to go to Nanaimo, to the shipyard."

The two men again walked away a few paces and bend their heads together in whispered consultation. Having come to an agreement they stepped back to the boat and said, "This is illegal, you are not allowed to operate this boat. You cannot leave, the boat must stay here." After this announcement they turned and sped up the dock towards the land presumably to report to their superior.

John Bevelander, the amazed skipper, watched them run up the ramp and enter a parked car. *Well I'll be*, he thought, *this is crazy*.

The phone rang in my office which at the time was located at the corner of Denman and Georgia Street.

"Hello," I said, picking up the phone.

"Hey Jan, I have just been told that I can't take the

boat to Nanaimo." He proceeded to inform me about his encounter with the two officials.

His report struck a familiar chord. A few days previous, Jules and I had come back from a short sail in *Lioness*. When we entered the harbour we spotted a large yacht tied up to one of the fuel barges. It was the *Shango*, a 140 foot yacht owned by a very wealthy American businessman. The yacht was operated by Gordon and Nanno Stout, a couple we knew from the Caribbean. Jules knew them very well since she had once hitched a ride with them from Gibraltar to the Caribbean. (This was before we met.)

Excited to see the boat, I checked *Lioness'* speed and moved within hailing distance of Shango. "Hello, *Shango*," shouted Jules. A door on the bridge deck opened and sure enough, there was Gordon. We tied up alongside and went onboard. We hadn't seen Gordon and Nanno for several years and were happy to reminisce about old times. Gordon explained that they were on a world cruise and would be leaving the boat in Vancouver for a refit. The owner had gone home and would join the yacht again when the work was completed. Gordon said that running into us was a stroke of luck because he and Nanno had purchased a house in Fort Lauderdale and they preferred to go home also rather than having to stay with the yacht while she was in the shipyard. Gordon asked me to oversee the work while he and Nanno would spend some time at home. This was a great opportunity for me to earn a fair bit of cash, so I happily agreed to the proposal. However, upon checking with shipyards and trying to find temporary moorage for the boat, I ran into all kinds of snags. The size of the work project needed clearance through customs. Customs would not give a permit; only emergency repairs were permitted to foreign vessels! The boat would have to be in bond and could not be moved by Canadian crew unless the foreign owner was on board. Moorage would not be made available. We ran into a colossal amount of red tape and bureaucracy. Gordon got fed up and moved the yacht to Seattle where over a million dollars was spent on the job. Money and jobs lost to Canadians. It was my understanding that this had to do with Canadians buying boats in the U.S., leaving them in U.S. registry and thereby foregoing to pay the import duty. Fair enough, but in my opinion this situation was completely different. The Canadian authorities didn't see it this way, and that was that.

I thought about what John Bevelander had told me and figured that since the two customs men had left the scene, maybe their verdict was just an idle threat; perhaps they were just throwing their weight around a little bit. I told John to cast off his lines and take off for Nanaimo, pronto.

Almost an hour went by and I had forgotten about the incident when the phone rang again. It was John Bevelander again. This time he called from the yacht.

"Hello Jan, it's me again, over."

"What's up? Got problems? Over." I thought something on the boat had malfunctioned.

"Just got a call from Vancouver traffic. They said that they had been instructed by Customs to tell me that I must return to the marina immediately. Over."

"Oh, shit, what the hell is going on? Where are you? Over."

"We just passed Point Atkinson. What do you want me to do? Over."

Envisioning Customs calling the Coast Guard and the RCMP and imagining shots being fired across the bow, I replied, "You'd better turn back. I'll meet you at the dock. Over and out."

When I arrived at the dock a Customs official with lots of gold braid stood waiting for me. The boat was just entering the marina. The man started talking to me but I asked him to wait until I had helped take the lines and secured the boat to the dock. When everything was ship shape, he approached me and said that he was an inspector with Customs. I introduced myself and told him that the yacht was under my management. "In that case," he said, "I'm fining you five hundred dollars and the yacht is hereby seized."

"What on earth for?" I asked.

"This is a foreign vessel which is not allowed to operate in these waters without the owner or his representative on board."

"But I am his representative, and through me, the skipper is his representative."

"That's illegal because the skipper is a Canadian."

"Gee man, that's ridiculous. Have you seen the unemployment statistics lately? They're really bad. This man is gainfully employed. If it wasn't for this boat, he wouldn't have a job. As a matter of fact, nor would I."

"That can't be helped. I am acting according to the law; it's my duty to inform you…" and again he told me that he was seizing the boat and fining me the ransom.

"Could you just wait a moment?" I asked. "I want to make a phone call. Come with me if you like."

He followed me as I stepped onboard one of the other boats. She was located in a boat house nearby. This was the 73 footer owned by the gentleman from Spokane. I selected a key and opened the door to the deck salon. I suggested the inspector take a seat in one of the comfy chairs situated in the luxuriously appointed accommodation. Distracted and puzzled by his surroundings he sat down. I picked up the shore phone which stood on the bar at the other end of the spacious salon and dialed the number of Peter Mandrell, the fellow who worked for the department of Development and Tourism. The phone rang once and was immediately answered.

"Peter, how are you? This is Jan de Groot. I've got a real problem here, I need your help."

I gave Peter a brief history of the recent developments. Peter gave me his undivided attention, asked me a few questions and then said. "I want you to call this number. It's the number of the Chief of Customs. Give me about fifteen minutes, because I want to talk to him first. I'll tell him that you'll be calling." Peter hung up and I sat down, keeping an eye on my watch. The inspector had overheard some of the conversation and new I would be calling his boss. He quietly sat in the comfy chair scanning his surroundings. Fifteen minutes went by and I picked up the phone again. I dialed the number and was connected to the Chief of Customs. Again I repeated my story.

"Yes, I have been briefed by Peter Mandrell. Most unfortunate. The law is not intended to put a stop to your kind of operation, however, strictly according to that law, the inspector is correct. Under the circumstances, it would be best if you pay the fine. Pay it by cheque and write on it 'Payable under protest' then write me a letter explaining the circumstances, and I'll deal with it. Is the inspector there?"

"Yes, he is right here with me."

"Okay, let me talk to him. I'll explain the situation to him and tell him to release the vessel."

I turned to the inspector and handed him the phone. He put the receiver to his ear and I heard him say, "Yes sir, of course sir, will do sir." He put down the phone and explained to me that he had been instructed to release the boat and would I please give him a cheque written out as explained by the Chief of Customs. I did as I was told.

Subsequently, John Bevelander took the boat to the Nanaimo Shipyard where the work was carried out. He arrived safely, with the yacht, in Mexico some weeks later.

Less than a month went by when I read a story in the Vancouver Sun, Vancouver's newspaper. The article stated that a big American motor yacht had been seized by Customs in Nanaimo. The owner of the yacht apparently owned a chain of hotels. The Mayor of Campbell River, anxious to boost the economy of his electoral district, had been trying to persuade the yacht's owner to extend his hotel chain to Campbell River. Also, the Mayor of Nanaimo proposed that he build a hotel in that city. The newspaper reported that finally an agreement had been reached; the man had promised to build a hotel in Campbell River and in Nanaimo. The happy outcome was celebrated on the yacht when she was tied up along side a dock in Nanaimo. The mayors from both cities were onboard together with various people from the media. Drinks were being served as onlookers watched the festivities from the dock. A reporter who stepped from the boat was approached by one of the onlookers. He said to the reporter, "That's a pretty good party, hey? What kind of drinks are they serving?" "Oh, I had a couple of good old American whiskeys," the reporter answered and continued on his way. "Is that so?" the onlooker said and then went to the nearest telephone. He called Customs in Victoria and explained that he was Custom's Officer So-and-So and wanted to know if the yacht had reported a quantity of whiskey on board when it entered Canada. Apparently the answer was "no", which is not unusual because liquor that is used for consumption on board is seldom reported or even questioned. Armed with this information the man climbed onboard the yacht, identified himself and demanded to see the owner. He promptly seized the vessel. And when he learned that the yacht was going to have some work done in the Nanaimo Shipyard he forbid the work and fined the owner. Needless to say, by the time things had been straightened out through protests from the two mayors, the yacht steamed away from Canadian waters never to return and the hotels were never built.

While the reason for this action differed from my dilemma, the common denominator is that customs officers can create on the spot chaos without regard for the consequences and without consultation with their superiors.

As recommended, I wrote a letter to the Chief of Customs and also sent copies to the Premier of the

Province and to Canada's Prime Minister. The only reply I received came a few months later from Customs in Ottawa. The letter said that while they understood my reasoning and concern and while under the circumstances I should not have been fined, the regulations were such that I could not be permitted to operate, manage, and maintain foreign flag vessels in Canada without the foreign owners on board. It was also illegal to carry out repair work without special permits and those would be granted for emergency repairs only. My cheque would be returned by separate mail in due course.

So that was the end of that and we were back to where we had started. The business was down the tube. For a while I was employing Americans to give me time to return the yachts to their respective owners.

One interesting note: A few weeks after all this happened I had a phone call from a gentleman who introduced himself as the assistant manager of the Port of Seattle, Washington, U.S.A.

"I understand you have an interesting business going there in Vancouver. You manage a bunch of yachts, I understand."

"Yes," I said, puzzled by his call.

"Hm, I see. I also understand that you have trouble operating it because of certain Canadian laws."

"You appear to be well informed." I said, wondering where this was leading to.

"Yeah, well, we have been following this with some interest and we want you to know that if you would consider setting up your operation here in Seattle, we will give you all the assistance needed. And we have no problems with you employing Americans on foreign yachts, nor do we object to you having these yachts maintained and repaired in American shipyards." Obviously, Americans have different ideas about boosting their economy.

Silly rules and silly laws. It never ceases to amaze me. As time passes more laws are invented. Smoking laws, drinking laws, seat belt laws, bicycle helmet laws. Laws only benefit two groups of society: bureaucrats and criminals. More laws, more bureaucrats. More laws, more opportunities for criminals. I would have thought that the years of prohibition would have taught us a lesson. The drinking didn't stop, instead it gave berth to organized crime. Al Capone would have been a nobody without prohibition. Today, the worst element in the dope world are the crime syndicates. Without the laws, dope would be cheap and most of the different varieties possibly not even manufactured. Without the laws there would be no profit in it, so why make it? Without the profit, the crime syndicates wouldn't be pushing dope on our kids. Without the laws, the crime syndicates would be out of business. Those people who are already hooked won't give it up anyhow, regardless of the price and the penalties. Instead they will steal or even commit murder to get their hands on the stuff. Make it readily available under supervision of medical personnel and other qualified people and the crime element would be eliminated. This, I believe, is the only reasonable chance of eventually reducing consumption. Instead, we are expanding and spending more money on law enforcement to fight a losing battle. In my opinion, the money would be better spent on rehabilitation.

We tend to say "there ought to be a law against this or

that," not realizing that as each law is put in place more bureaucrats are hired, resulting in higher taxes and each time taking away a little bit more from an individual's liberty. But, that's enough of that. Onwards to happier things.

It was on Bowen Island where I met Herb. And it was because of Herb that I ended up back in the charter business and back in the West Indies. Now my regular job as a marine surveyor is pleasantly interrupted by taking the odd party on a sailing trip in the Caribbean. For this, we charter a bareboat from one of the charter companies.

I met Herb, and his charming companion Emily, when he came to me for sailing lessons. Herb is in his seventies, full head of gray hair (he calls it blond), erect posture, and full of life. Emily, much younger (and she needs to be to keep up with Herb), is a petite and attractive looking lady. She has a tremendous personality and capably operates her own prospering employment agency.

Herb has been very successful in business. His company, now under management by his son, has been sold to an affiliated company for a handsome sum of money. Herb maintains he is still active in the company, in what function I am not sure, but he does do a lot of travelling and seems to have an unlimited expense account. I suspect that the son is a real smart cookie who encourages the trips to get Herb out of his hair. Most of Herb's 'business' trips appear to consist of participating in endurance runs in Eastern Canada, climbing in the Himalayas, expeditions to the Antarctic, and now, on a regular basis, sailing trips with me in the Caribbean.

Herb belongs to a mysterious society with a selective

and exclusive membership of four or five other corporate executives. They meet once a year in some exotic place where, after evaluation of the previous year's activities, an award is granted to the member who has had the most noteworthy (read that as 'bizarre') experience.

Last year the society was to meet in Singapore at a certain time on a certain date. Everyone arrived on time except Herb. A message conveyed to them by the hotel staff stated that Herb had been delayed and would be joining them soon. Three days later Herb arrived and joined the group. The meeting was called to order and Herb was asked to justify his delay. Herb offered his apologies and said that he had a legitimate reason. He had been detained by the dentist, had lost his dentures, and had been forced to wait until the dentist could fit him with a new set. When asked how he had lost his teeth, he explained that just prior to the meeting in Singapore he had attended a business meeting in a posh resort in the Bahamas. The entire resort had been reserved for the function. While seated in the vicinity of the swimming pool, he had been chatting with a few of the male attendees at the meeting. A considerable amount of liquor had been consumed when one of the fellows Herb was chatting with drew their attention to a well endowed and good looking lady who had entered the pool area, clad in a bathing suit that displayed great economy in use of material. The men observed her climbing the steps to the diving board and subsequently performing an elegant dive into the clear waters of the pool. She obviously enjoyed diving because she swam to the edge of the pool, climbed out, and once again ascended the diving board. After her second dive, Herb, slightly under the influence of the refreshments, exclaimed to his pals,

"Boy, wouldn't you like to take a bite out of that!"

"You wouldn't dare," said one of the other guys.

This was all the encouragement Herb needed.

"I wouldn't?" Herb answered. "Just you watch!" He got out of his seat and followed the lady up the rungs of the stairs when she climbed to the platform for the third time. Just as she stepped on the board, Herb's face connected with the lady's well formed derriere and Herb bit. The woman shrieked and leapt off the board into the water taking Herb's dentures, which were caught on her bathing suit, with her.

Herb's explanation earned him the coveted annual award which, as was confided to me by one of his cohorts, he had won on several occasions during previous years.

What has become a tradition on all cruises with Herb and Emily is the Rum Punch Survey. A great deal of time and effort is spent to arrive at an accurate appraisal of the quality of rum punches served throughout the islands. From year to year records are updated to ensure that certain standards are maintained. As we move from establishment to establishment the drinks are ordered and the first thing on the program is a close visual inspection of the contents. Notes are made in the appropriate ledgers kept in Herb's briefcase. Then, after some deliberation and delay, the time period of which depends on the amount of activity and drinks consumed just prior to the newly introduced variety, the first sip (or gulp) is taken. The glass is put down, the head slightly turned to an angle, a frown indicating deep concentration appears, and the lips are smacked. Then a remark:

"Hm, not bad, but I need to try some more for further assessment."

A rating based on a scale of one to ten is given during the next three sips. Sometimes the rating is changed as more drinks are consumed, usually upwards.

Herb is the undisputed expert in this and as a rule we will abide by his decision although the system is fairly democratic and Emily and I do have a certain amount of input, especially if the product rates closely to drinks served in another establishment.

At one time we were anchored at the Pitons in St Lucia and decided to go ashore to a place which demanded our rum punch expertise. The place had been recommended for investigation by other experts in the field. I won't mention the name of these public premises since we would like to keep it reserved for ourselves due to certain interesting discoveries. Suffice it to say that the place is located and well hidden against the hills of the Pitons. One of the attractive features is the seating arrangement. It is housed in a collection of small buildings with open sides and thatched roofs. The most memorable of these is one which is adorned with a crystal chandelier backed with a large Persian carpet. Initially we thought that the combination of these articles was a little out of place in that type of setting, but after further consideration it was decided that the structure and its contents had a certain charm. Towards one end of the square like area, around which the thatched buildings are located, a house has been constructed. It is of the Victorian style, adorned with gingerbread along the roof line and gaily painted in a variety of colours. In this building the kitchen is located and this is also where the drinks are prepared. A white man dressed in a long white robe could be seen occasionally fleeting in and out of the building and busying himself in the vicinity of a bamboo structure in which, as we found out, the toilet facilities are located. Doors were absent to these normally considered private areas.

After having taken in our surroundings with some amazement we found ourselves a table and chairs and sat down. The drinks were ordered and put on the table. Herb extracted the ledger from his briefcase and the contents of our glasses were studied. It had been a long climb up against the hill, so without wasting too much time a large gulp was taken. The glasses were put down and the lips were smacked.

"Wow," said Herb, "that hits the spot." He quickly picked up his glass again and this time drained it to the very bottom. "Waiter, another round please?" Turning to us he said, "What do you think? Well up there, don't you think? It has that certain pizzazz which I haven't encountered in any of the others."

"That's right," said Emily, "there is a slightly different taste to it. What is it?"

The next supply arrived and we delved in for further investigation.

"Don't know what it is," said Herb, "but whatever it is I'm beginning to like it more all the time." His second glass stood empty on the table. "Waiter, anodder round please." He looked at our glasses which still had plenty left. "Wasamatter, don't you like it? I think this is a twelve." He picked up the third glass which had been put in front of him. "Can't understand it, I think dis shtuff is getting to me."

"Waiter," this time Emily called the man who passed us with a tray full of glasses destined for an another table.

"Be right with you Ma'am," he answered.

The man returned. "What can I get you?"

"What are the ingredients in this rum punch?"

The man went into great detail about the recipe but nothing was mentioned that explained the distinctive taste. Herb was into his fourth drink and was singing. Emily and I felt giddy, too. The place was definitely attractive. That chandelier was spectacular and suited the place to a T. The Persian carpet was exquisite and probably thousands of years old, rare, priceless and probably not from this earth.

As we stumbled and sometimes slid down the hill, Emily suddenly stopped, sat down on a tree stump and said, "I've got it. It's hash. There's hash in those drinks. That's the taste we couldn't identify."

Rating: An undisputed twelve out of ten.

Herb prides himself on being understanding of the different ways in which service is provided in other parts of the world. 'When in Rome, do as the Romans do', is his favourite slogan. He repeats this quote often, too often, in my opinion, because it is usually said as a reminder to himself when things don't flow in the efficient, Western manner. In fact, regardless of all his travelling to different parts of the world, Herb has a short fuse when things don't go his way. He knows this and repeatedly checks himself when coming close to an outburst. His usual manner is to wipe his forehead with a handkerchief while saying to us, "Wow, wasn't I good? Did you notice that? I didn't say a thing. While in Rome do as the Romans do, that's my motto!"

Occasionally though, Herb slips up and is unable to contain his displeasure. He really got himself in a pickle on Union Island.

Herb, Emily, and I arrived just before darkness in Clifton Harbour, Union Island. We were on a boat that we had chartered from Barefoot Yacht Charters in St.Vincent. We had done a lot of sailing that day and were somewhat tired when we dropped the hook in the anchorage. We were sitting in the cockpit debating where to go for dinner when a large wooden dinghy operated by one of the Union Islanders stopped by and handed us a menu from one of the local restaurants. The man asked if we would like to make a reservation. The dinner featured lobster accompanied with entertainment from a group performing on steel drums. The fellow said he operated his boat as a water taxi and could pick us up and return us to our boat after dinner.

"What do you think?" Herb said to me, "Do you know this restaurant? Is it any good?"

I shook my head, "No, I've never been there."

"Sounds good though," Emily said, "Lobster and steel drums, sounds like fun. Using the water taxi makes sense too, because then we don't have to fret about putting the outboard motor on the dinghy."

I hadn't thought of that! While sailing, the outboard motor was taken off the dinghy and secured to the stern rail. It is a clumsy job, taking it off the rail, then stepping with it into the unstable dinghy and subsequently carrying it to the transom to secure it in position. As a rule, this job was delegated to me. "Yes, Herb," I said hopefully, "that makes a lot of sense. Let's go for the lobster and the water taxi."

"Well," Herb replied cheerfully, "if that's the wish of the Captain and the Admiral, the decision is made."

On all of our trips I was the Captain and Emily was referred to as the Admiral. Herb's position was somewhat unclear and varied from deckhand to first mate, depending on how he behaved. Often he was demoted or promoted due to some act during the trip. This was interrupted with promotion to the status of Minister of Finance when bills had to be paid.

At seven that evening, the man with the water taxi picked us up and took us to the restaurant. When we entered the establishment, I could tell by Herb's attitude that the place had not been a good choice. Definitely not Herb's style, and I must admit, neither Emily nor I were much impressed either. The large room was bare, lacking atmosphere, though the patrons were many and uncomfortably seated at long wooden tables with wooden benches. The band was loud and hollow sounding in the spartan surroundings. We were ushered to a section of the table where various other people were already consuming the fare.

The food turned out to be quite good and after a while with the encouragement of a regular flow of rum punch, the party was coming to life. Several people had moved to the dance floor. I figured we could hang around for a little while and then move to a more intimate place for a quiet drink. But that was not to be the case. When the plates were emptied, Herb paid the bill and looked around for the operator of the water taxi. He spotted him at the bar where he sat on a stool with a drink in his hand chatting with some of the other thirsty customers.

"We are ready to go back," said Herb to the man.

"You go back already?" he answered. "I just started a new rum punch." He grinned as he raised his glass to Herb and took a sip.

"Yes, we want to go back right now."

"Okay mon, relax," the man answered agreeably, "I'll be right dere, as soon as I finish my drink."

Emily and I looked at each other as we saw Herb's face flush and his mouth tighten. "Uh- oh," Emily whispered to me, "it's blow-up time." She had no sooner said this when Herb, still looking at his victim, straightened his back, stretched his neck lifting his chin, and said in no uncertain terms, "I said NOW! And I mean NOW, otherwise your services are no longer required, my friend!"

The boat man looked Herb over from tip to toe and replied, tipping the glass to his lips again, "No mon, not until I finish my drink. If you no like, too bad. I is de only game in town mon."

Herb rolled his eyes, shook his head and ushered us out of the restaurant. When we were outside, I said to Herb, "When in Rome, do as the Romans do."

"Oh, my God," said Herb, "I did it again, didn't I?"

"Yep," Emily agreed.

"But the guy was so insolent, imagine wanting to finish his drink first, we are his customers! Who does he think he is?" Herb argued.

"He's the only game in town," I said.

"Oh, no!" Herb uttered, "he wasn't kidding was he, are there no other boats? I have really done it this time, haven't I?"

Emily chuckled, "Yes, we are in for a long swim, Herb,

through shark infested waters."

Fortunately, I was able to locate Captain Janis, a friend of mine who operates a fleet of catamarans from Union Island. He took us safely back with one of the dinghies from his flotilla.

The control over Herb's fuse was admirable when another opportunity arose for him to receive an introduction into the West Indian way of dealing with problems.

This time we had chartered a boat from the Moorings in St. Lucia. Our voyage was to take us from St. Lucia to Grenada. Normally I arrange to arrive at the boat at least one day ahead of time. This allows me to check out the boat and get all the paperwork organized before my guests arrive. In this case, however, it turned out that all three of us, Herb, Emily and I, boarded a flight from Toronto to St. Lucia at the same time. The main airport in St. Lucia is located at the south eastern end of the island and from there it is a long trip by car over a windy road through mountainous terrain to the Marigot Bay location of the Moorings base. Herb had arranged for a helicopter to take us from the main airport to the smaller airport at Castries, thus eliminating the long ride with the taxi. As it happened, when we were about four hours into our flight from Toronto to St. Lucia, and while I was folded into my chair, head phones on my head watching the movie, the sound track was suddenly interrupted.

"This is the Captain speaking. You may have noticed that the sun has moved from the right hand side of the airplane to the left. This is because we have a small technical problem that cannot be fixed in St. Lucia.

There's is nothing to worry about, but we have been instructed to return to Toronto, so we have turned around and are on our way back."

It reminded me of the joke where the announcement came stating that the plane was now under full automatic control, everything was operating perfectly and there was nothing to worry about... worry about... worry about...worry about...

As luck would have it we did land without any problems, but after eight hours of flying we were back where we had started, in Toronto! Subsequently, another plane brought us to our destination, but we didn't arrive at the St. Lucia airport until well after midnight. The helicopter was now not available since it doesn't fly after sunset.

After a long taxi ride, we finally entered the lobby of the hotel-bar-restaurant-office of the Moorings in the wee hours of the morning. A lonely West Indian night clerk was on duty. We had arranged to stay in one of the Moorings cottages for two days prior to embarking on the yacht. After signing in, the clerk handed us the keys for the cottages and asked if we would like to have a complementary drink. We gratefully accepted and sat down, surrounded by our luggage, at a table in the reception area. Shortly after the drinks had been served, a staff member came to our table and offered to take us to our rooms and help with the gear. We had only just started to sip our drinks and if I knew Herb, he wouldn't be ready to move until he had downed at least one more. So I suggested that Herb and Emily relax with their drinks while I saw to the rooms and the luggage. The couple gratefully accepted.

I now have to explain the geographic location of the Moorings base. Marigot Bay consists of two bays, one behind the other. Its potential for naval warfare was explained in one of the earlier chapters when Sir Rodney managed to outwit the French fleet. The Moorings is located in the inner bay on the southern side. Their guest cottages are located along the southern shore line. The bay is surrounded by high, steep hills. Opposite of the Moorings base, on the north side of the bay is another establishment. It is called Dr. Doolittle's and named after the movie that was filmed there. I knew it well, because the movie's star, Rex Harrison, had been a guest on *Ring Andersen* during the filming. Dr. Doolittle's is situated against the mountain and encompasses a narrow peninsula that stretches out into the bay. Behind and above Dr. Doolittle's some dwellings are perched against the mountain. Some of these are holiday cottages which are operated by the Moorings when their own cottages are fully booked.

With the keys for both cottages in my pocket and straining under the load of luggage, I followed the guy who was also well laden with bags. To my surprise he went to the dock instead of following the path that lead into the direction of the Moorings cottages. When we arrived at the dock my guide started loading the suitcases and other paraphernalia into an open boat that was equipped with an outboard motor. I assumed that he had decided it was easier to cover part of the distance by boat and seated myself on one of the thwarts. When the fellow started the engine and the boat got underway, he set course for the opposite shore. Upon questioning him I discovered that apparently we had been assigned to a

Marigot Bay

A typcial local dwelling

cottage behind and above Dr. Doolittle's. When we arrived on the other side, the luggage was heaved on shore, collected by us, and once again I followed the fellow to our destination. We circled the bar and restaurant of Dr. Doolittle's, went up some steep steps, went along another path and then came to a platform from which a narrow gauge railroad track led steeply up the hill. The man put the luggage down, pressed a button on a pole and we waited. I tried looking along the tracks toward the top of the mountain but was unable to see anything except total darkness. After what seemed eternity, I noticed a contraption on wheels slowly coming down the tracks. It came to a stop at the platform. It had two seats, one opposite the other, a roof, and between the seats, some space for luggage. By the time our gear was onboard, there was only standing room for us two carriers. The man pushed the 'up' button on the pole and with a jerk our vehicle started its ascent. Slowly pulled by a heavy cable, it crawled upwards along the tracks. It came to a jerky halt when reaching the upper platform where I could see a small shack containing the electric winch. We unloaded the bags and went on our way along another path, a good fifteen minute walk, then up a few steps, down a few steps, onto another path, a turn, and there it was, a duplex cottage! Painted white, grown over with bougainvillea, and other tropical flowers, perfumed scents wafted along a patio with a small swimming pool overlooking all of Marigot Bay, including its mouth opening into the Caribbean Sea: magnificent! My companion offered to move the luggage into the building but I told him not to bother. "Just leave it here on the patio. Why don't you go and get the other two people

In the Bequia channel.
From left to right: the Minister of Finance,
the Admiral, the Captain.
Photo: Tim Wright

and bring them up here while I sort this out."

As the fellow departed, I absorbed a few minutes of the awesome scenery, especially impressive under the star and moon lit sky, and then took the key to my side of the duplex and opened the door. After I had moved my gear inside I put the key into the lock of Herb and Emily's accommodation. I turned the key, but the lock did not respond. I fiddled with it until I realized that I definitely had the wrong key. I tried my key; it wouldn't work either. I sat down by the pool and waited for the rest of the party to arrive.

"Wow, what a trip," Herb puffed as he stepped onto the patio. Emily followed right behind him.

"Where's the guy who brought you up here?" I asked.

"Herb sent him on his way," Emily answered, "Why?"

"The key to your cottage doesn't fit. They gave us the wrong key."

"Oh well," Herb declared cheerfully, "why don't you guys stay here while I go back to the desk to get another key. Then I can pick up another rum punch along the way."

"Are you sure, Herb?" I asked.

"Yes, absolutely, no problem, I'll be right back."

With the key clasped in his hand Herb stepped off the patio, made the turn along the path, up a few steps, down a few steps, then further along the long path until he came to the platform. The cable car was not there since it had been taken down by the Moorings attendant. Herb pushed the button and waited until the unit arrived. He stepped on board, pushed the button and slowly descended down along the face of the mountain. When he arrived at the bottom and plodded along to Dr.

Doolittle's he noticed a black man coming toward him.

"Hello," Herb said, "do you work here?"

"Yes, sir!" the man answered, "I is de guard."

"Ha, good," Herb said, "I wonder if you could help me. You see, I am in cottage number 26 and I have been given the wrong key. I wonder if you could go to the Moorings and exchange this key for the right one."

"Sure boss, de key she don't fit?" He took the key from Herb and studied it. A tag, attached to it was labeled '26'. He looked at the tag, turned it over in his hand and turned it back to the side that displayed the number. Questioningly he looked up at Herb.

"But dis is de right key, see?" he showed the number to Herb.

"I know that's what it says, but it doesn't fit."

Not believing Herb the guard shook his head, "I show you," he said and still shaking his head, and with Herb following, he walked up the path toward the platform of the cable car. It so happened that the thing was still where Herb had left it, so they climbed in, the guard pushed the button and up they went. Slowly they moved upwards along the tracks. When they reached the upper platform, they stepped out, walked along the long path, went up a few steps, down a few steps and went further along the path that curved toward the cottage. The guard put the key into the door lock and turned it. Nothing happened. Again he twisted the key, this way and that way, but to no avail. He pulled the key out of the lock, studied it and said, "She don't fit, dis de wrong key."

"Yes," said Herb, "better go to the desk and get the right one." Herb turned to us putting both hands to his head, "I told him, the thing doesn't fit. He wouldn't believe me." As the guard departed, Herb suddenly said, "Better make sure he comes back, I better go with him." Herb took off after the guard. He caught up to him when he had come to the end of the path that turned away from the cottage. Up a few steps, down a few steps and on they walked to the platform. The conveyor was still there. Onboard they climbed, the button was pushed and slowly they crept down the mountain. Then out at the lower platform, a stiff walk past Dr. Doolittle's, into a dinghy tied to the dock, across the bay, a climb up the shore to the hotel lobby, then onwards to the desk. Both of them confronted the clerk.

"This is the wrong key. I can't get into my cottage." The guard stood alongside Herb, agreeing.

The clerk took the key, examined it and looked at the tag. He looked into a compartment of a shelve fastened against the wall behind him, shook his head and said,

"Dere no oder key, dis de right key mon. Look at de tag she say 26." Shaking his head he put the key in his pocket and left the lobby with Herb and the guard following. Down to the boat they went, across the bay they motored, then along the path past Dr. Doolittle's, around the buildings, another climb up the next path until they came to the platform. Someone else had used the carrier. It was at the top of the mountain. They pressed the button and waited for it to come down.

Emily and I had started to investigate the security of the windows in the building. I found a window that with some persuasion could be forced open. Emily rummaged through her valises and produced a shoe horn. I went to work and after some pushing and shoving, the window opened. I climbed in and was able to disengage the door lock from the inside. We moved the luggage inside and Emily started to unpack.

In the mean time, the trio of clerk, guard, and Herb was slowly being hoisted along the railway towards the summit. Upon their arrival, they stepped out of the vehicle and started the fifteen minute stretch along the well trodden path, then up a few steps, down a few steps, and then onto the curved path towards the patio of the cottage.

The clerk stuck the key into the lock and turned it. Nothing happened. He pulled it out, looked at it and put it in again. Some more twisting followed. Then he said, "Dis key, she don't fit, dis de wrong key!"

We sent the guard and the clerk on their way with the message that we would pick up the correct key in the morning, if it could be found.

Amazingly, Herb never lost his good mood during the entire exercise. When I asked him if he was feeling all right, he answered, "When in Rome, do as the Romans do."

The next day Herb was again waiting at the lower platform for the contrivance to come down. One of the chamber maids was also waiting.

"Boy, it takes a long time for that thing to come down," Herb remarked to the lady.

The woman looked up at Herb and said with a gentle smile on her face,

"She come when she come, and no-ting can be done."

Intrigued by this wisdom and hoping for more, Herb continued the conversation.

"Do you work here?"

"Yes, I work here for six years now."

"Really, are you married?"

"Yes, I is, and I has two children."

"Two children? Wow! And how old are they?"

"De boy be sixteen and de girl fourteen now."

"Sixteen and fourteen," exclaimed Herb, "you don't look old enough to have children that age!"

"Yes," the lady answered laughingly, "de age be old, and de body be old, but de face be young."

That evening I decided to look up my old friends Pat and Nick, ex operators of the yacht *Cariad* and now the owners of the Bistro, a restaurant in Rodney Bay. To get across to the Moorings base where I would be able to find a taxi, I took the ferry which regularly plies between the south side of the bay and Dr. Doolittle's. The ferry is a small barge with seats and a canvass awning that provides accommodation for about ten persons. It is powered by an outboard motor and operated by a St. Lucian in his late teens. When I arrived at the Moorings base I asked the clerk to call me a taxi. Rather than waiting for it to appear, I decided to start walking in the right direction, which is up a fairly steep hill and then along a road that partially circles the bay. I enjoyed the walk and the scenery. The inland side of the road is lined with quaint, West Indian houses made of rough wood, windows with decorated shutters, lots of ginger bread and dolled up in a variety of colours. I exchanged greetings with the inhabitants as they were working in the gardens or relaxing in their front porch.

As I continued along the road, suddenly, seemingly out of nowhere, an old lady appeared from behind the

She offered me a lily

lush vegetation of bushes and a trees on the higher embankment adjacent to the road. She was holding onto the trunk of a tree with one hand while she reached out to me with the other. In her hand she had a flower, a white lily. The back of her thin frame was bent with age. She was dressed in a long dark skirt, a white blouse, a loosely fitting cardigan, a shawl covering her head, and wearing a somewhat crooked, toothless smile on her angular and wrinkled face. I stopped in my tracks and stared at the apparition slightly elevated above me on the high embankment, not knowing what she wanted. Again she proffered the flower, hinting I should take it. With hesitance I stepped forward and took it from her hand. "Thank you ma'am, thank you very much." Instead of answering, she gave a shrill cackled laugh, somewhat wicked I thought, turned around and disappeared into the bushes. Her behaviour gave me a chilled feeling When later I related my encounter to Pat and Nick, they hinted that probably a voodoo curse had been put upon me. Fortunately, so far no great catastrophic event has crossed my path; therefore, I assume that the lady's gesture was made in friendship and not to cast a nasty spell.

Still standing on the road, twirling the flower's stem in my hand, I spotted the taxi coming toward me, driving slowly over the bumpy road. I waved and got in. After a half hour drive I was seated at the Bistro, reminiscing with Pat and Nick about old times and voodoo curses.

It was close to eleven P.M. when I walked up the dock to catch the ferry back to Dr. Doolittle's. The operator stood at the landing site, scanning the bay which was enveloped in darkness, but his craft was nowhere to be seen.

"Where's the ferry?" I asked.

"She gone, " the young man answered in a desperate tone. He was obviously in a bit of a state. "I was washing she down and when I feenish I put de broom and de bucket back in de shed. When I come back, de ferry she gone. I tink somebody borrow she."

"Holy smokes," I uttered, "But where did it go? It can't go very far, it's got to be somewhere in the bay. Nobody in his right mind would dare take that thing outside into the open sea."

As we both scanned the bay, he mumbled something incomprehensible in reply. Then we saw it, a vague, dark silhouette, barely distinguishable against the sky, in the outer bay toward the sea. We should have heard the engine running, but we didn't. "Maybe you didn't tie it up properly and it drifted away," I suggested.

"No, I tie she up good, somebody borrow she," he said again, looking at me, not knowing what to do.

"Borrowed it?" I questioned, "That's an interesting way of putting it." I thought for a minute, pondering the problem. "There's a dinghy with an outboard motor at the Moorings, " I suggested. "Let's go and BORROW it!"

My proposal produced a big smile on the boy's face. Before long we put-putted through the anchorage to where the ferry was located. It was slowly drifting out to sea. There were two men onboard. Apparently they were known to the ferry operator. The cover had been taken off the engine. A heated discussion started when we boarded. I left them arguing and fiddling with the ferry's motor, while I tied a line to its bow and attached it to the dinghy. I towed the ferry to the Dr. Doolittle's landing site and tied both crafts to the jetty.

I could still hear the trio arguing when I ascended the mountain, seated in my chariot, slowly being hauled up the steep tracks. The scent of tropical flowers drifted through the air while a faint, warm breeze rustled the dense foliage around me. As I rode further up against the mountain I could see the water like a black mirror in the bay, and further out, I saw the dark shadows of the swells steadily marching across the ocean. I looked up at the starlit sky and reflected upon the events of the past twenty-four hours. I listened to the crickets and the tree frogs whose whistles and chirping now drowned out the voices of the men on the ferry.

It was good to be back in the Caribbean.

Epilogue

The yacht charter business in the West Indies was started by Commander Nicholson. Retired from the British Navy, he and his family sailed across the Atlantic in their sailing yacht and settled in Antigua in the 1950's. The Commander began chartering his yacht shortly after their arrival, initially as a part-time endeavour which soon gained in popularity. From this, Nicholson Yacht Charters was born. The firm is now operated by the family's sons, daughters and grand children. Their base is located in English Harbour, Antigua. English Harbour is the site of Nelson's dockyard and has been fully restored. The area is administered by the Friends of English Harbour, an historical society. It is now one of the main attractions in Antigua and might have been passed over unnoticed had it not been for the efforts of the Nicholson's.

Another person who made life a lot easier for the charter operators is Don (Squeeky) Street, who in the early days conned his sailing yacht *Iolaire* into every nook and cranny throughout the islands and produced updated charts and cruising guides. They were of great help to the charter operators, especially the new arrivals. Don is also the local Insurance Broker and has been looking after the yachties' insurance needs for many years. Author of several books about yachting, I am pleased to note that both Squeeky and *Iolaire* are still in good health and still exploring the islands. Others have followed in Don's footsteps. Chris Doyle's cruising guides come as a complementary copy with most bareboat charters and are kept as treasured keepsakes of the trip.

Bob Smith was the first to organize and set up a central booking office for charter yachts. His company, 'Charter Services', is located in St.Thomas and looks after the bookings and administration of the yachts operating in the Virgin Islands. Bob and his wife went back to the USA in the late seventies after leaving the operation in the capable hands of ex charter yacht operator Kathy Mullen.

Some others of the old gang that are still in the islands are:

Jol Byerly, ex skipper of the yacht *Lord Jim*. He is now a yacht broker and operates Nicholson Yacht Sales in English Harbour.

Hazen Richardson, ex charter yacht operator and now owner of the exclusive Petit St. Vincent (PSV) resort. A few years back he celebrated his twenty-fifth anniversary on the island.

Kurt and Sheila Barts with their yacht *Nirvana*, to my knowledge, are the only complete team of the original cast, still chartering. Their yacht remains in meticulous condition and is based in the Blue Lagoon in St. Vincent.

Note: Just prior to going to press, Kurt passed away due to lung disease. You'll be missed Kurt! Sheila is anticipating her next step while staying with friends in Bequia. Our thoughts are with you, Sheila!

Afrikaner Frick Potgieter, skipper of the yacht *Mizar*, known as the man who wrestles sharks and who I once caught chasing ants on *Mizar* with an injection needle containing poison, has returned to Grenada. He and his wife and two beautiful children have become landlubbers and they bought a house just outside of St. George's. When we visited recently, Frick mentioned how often he and several other skippers had talked about the need to write a book about our various exploits. He said, "We talked about it many times but it never came to anything. I'm so glad you have done it. It's well overdue!"

So there, guys and gals, I've tried my best and hope it meets with everyone's approval.

The following is a list of some of the magnificent yachts that plied the Caribbean while engaged in the charter trade during the seventies.

Name of Yacht	Present Status (sometimes rumoured, not entirely reliable)
Alianora	Seen in Fort Lauderdale, 1995
Anna Marie	Shipwrecked
Anna Lisa	Unknown, last seen in the Mediterranean
Antares	Reported shipwrecked
Ariels	Shipwrecked
Cariad	Reported to be in Europe
Celestial	Unknown
Circe	Unknown
Clover	Spotted in Newport Beach, CA, 1992
Dana	Shipwrecked
Peter Storm	Shipwrecked
Buccaneer	Shipwrecked
Dixie	Shipwrecked
Eudroma	Unknown
Fair Cera	Unknown
Fair Carol	Shipwrecked
Fandango	Unknown
Flicka	Unknown
Freelance	Shipwrecked
Free Spirit	Unknown
Gitana	Unknown
Grace	Reported shipwrecked
Harbinger	Sighted in St. Lucia, 1993
Hurricane	Lying in Union Island, no longer chartering

Jacintha .... Shipwrecked, reported to have a
ghost on board
Janine .... Unknown
Kalizma .... Unknown
Kittiwake .... Unknown
Lord Jim .... Last seen on West Coast US,
early 1990's
Lunaquest .... Unknown
Makrele .... Unknown
Margay .... Unknown
Marie Pierre .... Unknown
Maverick .... Unknown
Mocambo .... Unknown
Naraina .... Unknown
Night Wind .... Unknown
Orphee .... Reported in the Virgin Islands
Panda .... Destroyed by fire in
Martinique
Ring Andersen .... Recently back, chartering in
the West Indies
Sea Biscuit .... Unknown
Shango .... Unknown
Snark .... Unknown
Sirocco .... Unknown
Storm Vogel .... Unknown, last seen in the
Med.
Tamilla .... Unknown
Topaz .... Shipwrecked
Thor Helga .... Unknown
Ticonderoga .... In good condition, still cruising
Tiki .... Unknown
True Love .... Unknown
Vanda .... Derelict in Grenada, 1995
Zorra .... Unknown

Cargo vessels operated by yachties

Hildur .... Scrapped in Grenada
Jens Juhl
(sailing cargo vessel) .... Reported shipwrecked
Sonja .... Status unknown
Fantasy .... Reported shipwrecked

The Author and his pal William

About the Author

Jan de Groot has roamed the world on merchant ships and yachts. Now a Canadian citizen, he is a regular contributor to various magazines of short stories and articles about the sea and boating. Other books under his name are: *Buying the Right Boat, Tips and Tricks for Boaters* and *No Shoes Allowed.* He is currently working on *Raven's Story*, the amazing account of the sailing ship *Raven* that ever since her construction in 1929 was haunted by a ghost. The vessel's eventual destruction on an uncharted reef near Isle de la Gonave is shrouded in mystery and came close to creating an international incident between Haiti and the USA.

If you want to contact the author, or order more books for your friends, send e-mail to degroot@axionet.com.